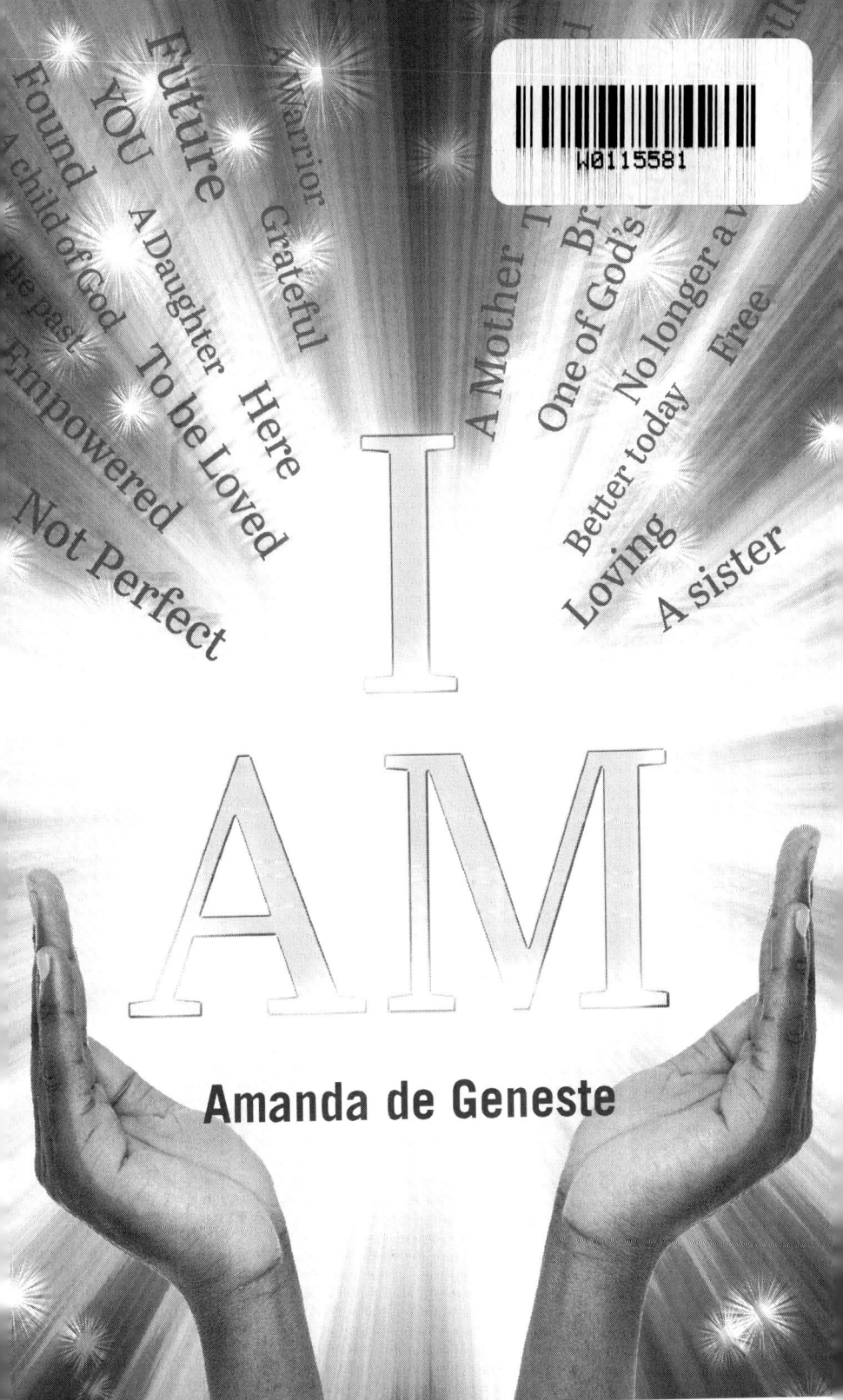

Photography: Roger "Phaats Photo" Archer
Illustration: Jassim R. Thomas

ACKNOWLEDGEMENT

To my brothers and sisters, Jeneva, Alice, Victor, Althea, Norman, Everist, Wesley, Jasmine and Linnie: There are no words to express how blessed I am to have you all as siblings. Each of you played an instrumental part in the building of my character to be who I am today. I will forever be grateful.

Jasmine and Victor, your unwavering encouragement and support has brought me to and through this part of my journey. Thank you for always believing in and loving me, in your own special way.

To my children, Orlanzo, Mike, Tiffany, Angel and my niece-daughter Curissma: God could not have given a more diverse and amazing set of personalities to have to set an example for. Your presence in my life keeps pushing me closer to understanding, compassion and achievement. I have learned and gained so much from the love you all have for me.

To friends Wendell Stratford and Family: Your thoughtfulness in seeing the need to help unearth that which stifled me played a major part in the accomplishment of "I AM". From the bottom of my heart, I appreciate you.

To my prayer warriors, Fermin & Dameris Archer, Chasity Slade: Thank you for your prayers and your prayerful guidance through this part of my journey.

POETIC "REPRIEVE"

The people, experiences, and things that shapes our lives—moments that have broken us, moments that have helped to put us back together—our foundation, the experiences of hardship, grief, love, disappointments, losses, and gains; laughter and prayer.

God said to Moses, "I AM WHO I AM." And he said, "Say this to the people of Israel: "I AM has sent me to you" Exodus 3:14

I am to know that I am full of *life*, full of *love* but most of all, full of *God*!

DEDICATION

This book is dedicated to my daughter Ayannah Gaynelle, my father Norris Isadore, my mother Stella Emelda (I speak for you also) and the millions of victims silent or free! If you are carrying painful, long held stories and the stench it has left within you, this is especially for you. Watch karma shift, "Let it out!"

CONTENTS

INTRO

I start this part of my journey by saying, "If I am to meet my maker today, right now, this moment, I will be okay with that." Am I afraid to die? Absolutely, I don't know when, where, or how it's going to happen and I guess that's what makes me afraid. Not the being dead part of course, because when it is all said and done, I won't feel any more of the pain in this world. It will be the people whose lives have touched mine with their love, who will then need to accept that I'm no longer with them physically, and that will be very sad. It usually is, when you lose someone you love.

I say it will be okay because I have literally been through hell and back several times and I AM still standing today, willing to make the round trip again mentally, I'm not sure though if I'm able to physically but I feel that I AM. That is how strong my faith in God is. I know he has carried me through some of the worst times that anyone has had to go through. Even if it meant leaving a little piece of me, I have come through these times standing on my own two feet able to walk away and able to smile in the face of other things life throws at me, sometimes even laugh. I AM smiling right now actually, smiling because I AM here with the mental and physical capacity to be able to share some of my journey with you through pen and paper. That is truly a miracle—I truly don't know where I'm going; the only thing I know for sure is where I came from and how I got here—God!

I was born in the country of Trinidad and Tobago, the West Indies. At the age of eleven I was brought to live in the United States of America. By the time I was fifteen, my mother pulled me out of high school because of non-attendance, all due to my difficulties adjusting to my new environment. Weeks later, I took it upon myself to register at the high school in the district where I resided. As it turned out, that didn't work well for me either. That chain of events led to my pregnancy at a very young age, which I touch upon later. Since then, I was able to educate myself; start and end a career I loved, in law enforcement; got married; raised three, sometimes extremely thoughtful, very supportive, wonderful children; and have also been widowed.

It hasn't been easy, but without a doubt it has been quite a journey, one I would like to share because I believe a testimony of my experiences can help some of my readers. Through my journey I have learned, it helps to know there are others who have traveled similar paths. People who are not just still standing but standing strong on their own two feet, willing to proceed on their journey with the 100 percent they have left inside of them. My journey continues.

CHAPTER 1

Remembering

I watched as she busied herself at the sewing machine, she was excited, which made me excited, I was no older than four years old. After what seemed to be only a matter of minutes, I was dressed and in the arms of my father. My mother was born in Trinidad and she was what Trinidadians called a "Dougla" (a person of mixed African and East Indian subcontinent descent)—her father was half-Chinese and half-African, and her mother was East Indian. I was dressed to go on an adventure with my father and she was happy, she smiled at me and waved goodbye. My mother assisted the family financially by working as a seamstress, not only did she sew all of our clothing, curtains and cushion covers, she also sewed clothes for other people.

During the trip with my father, I felt nauseous sitting on his lap while on the bus. I suffered from what I now know to be motion sickness. At the time, people including my parents were unaware of such things. Instead one coped and either tried to overcome these types of things or avoided the things that caused them. As a result, unbeknownst to my parents, I suffered through it. I do not recall where I went with my father. What I do remember, however, is that on the way home, I sat on his lap in a taxi. The wind was blowing into the window when I decided to spit through the window, the spit flew back into the car, directly in my father's face! Oops! He gave me *the look*, pulled out his handkerchief and wiped his face. I remember feeling bad but that is all I can recall about my very first memory. I imagine I must have been no older than three or four years old. Children that young can remember—some of those memories are vague at times but some are vivid. This memory, although sharp, I have no recollection of our destination, probably because it was normal for me to sleep through my motion sickness when it became too overwhelming.

At that time, in Trinidad we were a family of eleven, nine siblings plus my parents. My memories of it all include laughter, love, madness, togetherness, and pain. We had all the essential elements, which was as close to normal as we could have been for such a large family living in the West Indies.

Through God, my father Norris Isadore de Geneste, my sister Alice, and my mother Stella Emelda Hemlee-de Geneste, I learned pride, self-preservation, and resilience. Sure, I learned things that were not so good but I also made a choice to leave those not so good things in the *not so good and bad things box.*

I learned how to give love and how to forgive. From it all, I developed dignity, strength, and a forgiving heart. I would like to think that there is some common ground of thought where we know right from wrong, good from bad, intentional from unintentional, honest from dishonest, and fortunate from unfortunate. I sum it up as, "My life, despite all of its trials and tribulations has been tough but it has been a great life, I AM one of the fortunate people."

Every bit of my past is special in some way. When I look back, I think of the saying, "Less is more". We had so little financially but what we couldn't buy we made, and what we bought we shared. Sharing the little we had amongst so many helped to build a great sense of appreciation for things others took for granted. Imagine being a large family of eleven and one of the Christmas desserts includes two apples imported from the United States. Two, because after buying the necessities to feed us all we could barely afford much more. Those two apples were used for two servings, one apple was sliced into eight sometimes ten pieces. We gathered around as it was sliced, waiting to receive our portion of that *apple*. Trinidadians that have never been to America could not resist the aroma and the taste of a *Red Delicious apple*. It is a memory which will never, ever fade. Needless to say, when I arrived in this wonderful country, my favorite snack for many years was apples. When I received my 25 cents allowance each week, I'd run to the produce stand to purchase a 5-pound bag of apples for a quarter, yes, a quarter. Heaven it was!

Even the horrifying parts of my life, the abuse and molestation that I am now writing about has produced in me, a better listener and the empathy needed for the victims I came in contact with during my career in law enforcement. I have even developed a special type of courage, after all here I AM about to share some of the things that have shaken my existence to the core. I AM still standing, able to smile on most days and hoping to help others on their journey.

During my life many people have said, "You should write a book!" This statement is the result of their listening to me share different incidents in my life. When I sat and thought about my experiences, I said to myself, "Yes, I should write a book, but who would want to read a book that I would write?" No one knows who I am; no one cares about my experiences, when they are dealing with their own. Then I realized, how I wish someone, anyone had been forthcoming and shared what I will be writing about—child molestation, sexual abuse, rape, and physical abuse. The secrets held onto by so many who have suffered the very same things I will write about, which have caused so much damage internally. Some of the damage recognized and some not, causes a painful domino effect to themselves and the people close to them. It really is never too late to share because it helps us cope better mentally and emotionally. Who doesn't want to be better each day? I know I do. I AM striving to be a better me each day.

"Family"

I remember when I was a little girl.

Can you remember when you were just a little girl or a little boy?

Listening to Christmas Carols and can't fall asleep because you were eager to know who got what toy.

The importance of Christmas cake,

Leaving the children with cake batter, never again that mistake she will ever make.

Cake batter mixing and fingertips dipping till batter no more,

Oh, how she cried seeing that empty bowl, when she returned from the store.

The pet parrot always being chased, hobbling all through the house.

Children stealing condensed milk from inside the refrigerator, I crept out of the kitchen as if I were a mouse.

Father whistling Christmas Carols all through the Season,

Shortages of money but an abundance of love without conditions

No bread would we buy, so many mouths to be fed.

Flour, she bought and kneaded then voila! Nothing like hot buttered homemade bread.

Then there's that trip we would take together, to dad's job on Father's Day

All nine siblings holding a gift for him, for days on his job he would stay

Oh, how I missed those special and wonderful days

Slicing and sharing an apple into eight pieces

Enjoying the taste and the aroma of the Red Delicious

This is a piece of the story about the family called the de Geneste.'

Each day seemed like a summer vacation, the weather consistently warm in the seventies and better. The sun beaming down most days. There are two seasons there, the rainy season and the dry season. On sunny days when we didn't have school, we were playing out in the backyard. When our father wasn't working, he would be laying on his bed in front of the television, windows open enjoying the wonderful breeze as he read his newspapers. Oftentimes, whistling while reading. Relaxing and listening to the happenings of all his children and his wife. He was no doubt very family-oriented. At the time, I was the second to the last of nine children. There was Jeneva, Alice, Victor, Althea, Norman, Everist (whose nickname was Erna), James (whose real name is Wesley); and yes, there are stories behind the names, which could be an entire book on its own. Then there was me (Gail or Abby as my grandfather called me) and finally, Lisa (better known now as Jasmine). In 1971, my mother departed for the United States of America, it was a very sudden move. So sudden, that it took us all off guard, including my father.

My father said, "Someday you will be a news reporter," as he laid there reading his newspaper. I asked him, why he was crying? "Your mother left to go to America, your grandfather knew and paid for her to go, but they didn't tell me until the last minute." I was about six years old at the time, I don't recall feeling any pain, but I could see he was hurting. I didn't quite understand what was happening. She left, our Mom left. A year earlier, my oldest sister Jeneva had gone to Canada, where she stayed with a cousin. I am not sure what prompted my mother to leave. I'd like to imagine, she was encouraged by the dream of belonging to the Land of Opportunity "America!" Thinking back though, raising nine children in all of that madness she probably needed to breathe and didn't even realize it. She wasn't out of our lives completely. I sensed she would be back. She migrated to the United States so we, all of us, could have an opportunity at a new and better life. She left my father and seven of her young children— ranging in age from eighteen to four and a half years old. Almost seven years later, I saw her again. During that time we wrote to each other, but I didn't see her again until I was ten years old. In my letters, I usually requested that she send me books to read and she did; it meant the world to me. In my letters, I usually requested that she send me books to read and she did, which meant the world to me. I remember missing her, not literally but the notion of a mom not being there. She was, what we would refer to today as a crazy black woman, overwhelmed with her responsibilities, but I don't think she knew what being overwhelmed meant. I know she was missed by my father and some of my older siblings, but there was also an appreciated calmness in her absence that we all felt, including our father.

My mother, as beautiful as she was on the outside was as physically and verbally abusive to us when she was younger. As she aged, I often heard her admit to her abusive ways with remorse. Looking back, I remember always functioning in fear. In our household, fear came before respect. So, when I say we were conditioned to perform in a certain way, let's just say that I am most calm when I am under pressure. Most people at that time thought, when something traumatic took place in a child's life they got past it because they wouldn't remember it later. I am evidence that this is not true. I did not get past it, I remember. I learned to live with it and mask my fear along with my pain. The molestation I endured took place during the time my mother was away. A lot of what I have been through, I often think if she were around it would have never happened because she was my "mom" that crazy black woman. My mom would have sensed it, and if not, then the mere presence or thought of her insane sometimes uncontrollable behavior would have been a deterrence to even my ugliest monster

"Mom"

You planted the seed

Resilience is what you taught me,

To stand tall at five foot two.

Never regret anything you have done in your life is what you told me,

Now you don't even know me but if I could go back, this is what I would do

Just so this feeling inside me; my love for my mother,

you would see how much of it I hold inside for you.

As you have loved me in your own way.

Sporadic moments of spewed utterances, and speeches you gave

For my sake of assurance "Love you Baby" is what you would always say.

Trying as most mothers do, to give a crash course on lessons of things deemed most important to give to their child

If I could go back I would show more of my love for you before your memory, your mind with me in it would die.

Give you a love you would feel even through the loss of your memory of me

A love filled with resilience, passion for compassion, ambition to not just strive.

Mom, if I could go back, I would pay attention to that phrase Dad always said, "Once a man, twice a child."

If I could go back, I would Love you like someday I may lose you through the loss of the precious memories of me, you hold in your mind.

I remember!

During the time she was gone, my sister Alice was my father's right hand. Although only in her late teens, she graciously accepted her role and did a mighty fine job. I was too young to understand the actual extent of Alice's entire responsibilities or to understand that my mother left with the hope of making a better life for her family but not too young to appreciate the quiet her absence brought. I was introduced to a new way of life. Very obedient and every movement made was upon being told. We were, as some would say, "Well trained." Of course, not a term I appreciate now but I had an understanding of what was meant. We were taught to be respectful of others, to be polite, and to demonstrate good manners. We were taught dignity, ambition, and empathy. Behaviors that are all too absent in most children being raised today. Traits I still appreciate enough to pass on to any child that grows up around me. I am and will, however, always be mindful of the way I define the act of what I give them to take through their lives, and not "train" them but teach them.

I sometimes wonder what effect it had on Alice to this day! Although she seems to have it altogether, with what life experiences have thought me, I imagine she continues to wear a mask because she was never taught to do anything other than that. I love her dearly for the involuntary sacrifices she made and the strength she continues to demonstrate. I am hoping, if she hasn't already, she takes a moment at some point to let go of some or all of the hurt she feels from the experience.

Psalms 59:9 "Because of his strength I will watch for you, For God is my stronghold." She did, to the best of her ability …

"Thank You"

Please don't say a word, let me.

You brushed my knee and blew what I thought was the pain away, not one but oh, so many days.

Each time you look at me I felt you pray,

God let her not be led astray and I hope she has a better day.

Watching over me sometimes smothering my curiosity,

Sometimes in your own world or at a distance

But always looking to the side glancing at me

Trying hard to have patience through my journey.

It hasn't been easy for you, I know, but with great reward, upon us earnestly bestowed the blessing of seeing each other grow old.

Today, for just a moment, I shall time it.

Rest my sisters and my brothers; your heads my shoulders, such a great fit.

Oh sister you have so been like a mother,

The rest of you like no other brother or sister

All of your love for me has never failed.

Rest your head on my shoulders and for one moment exhale.

I have come to this day bringing a part of each of you within me.

You need not look behind anymore for your little sister Abby

For, now strong in faith and on the same path are we.

Your weight of me now lessened I hope,

As we are now side-by-side being each other's company.

To guide, pull, and sometimes carry the offspring of both you and me ...

Rest one moment, for once, Do as I say,

Breathe in, then exhale, we've come a long way.

At least a few moments without worry I'll take the reins

Don't worry; trust me I will do as you taught me, your teachings were not in vain.

Hear me as you stand before me today

Listen to my words, and see the passion, in which I say,

No better time than now, know this is a fact

I must accomplish this before you or I lay breathless on our backs.

I come cheek-to-cheek and head to head with you while sharing a breath together

Please hear me in this moment as I whisper

"THANK YOU for being Great brothers, Sisters and one hell of a Sister Mother!"

In 2001, as my father laid in the hospital hooked up to a ventilator, I took his hand and placed it in mine. He lived a long, hard but good life. He was not a very affectionate person and considering where he came from his efforts were great. I have always been proud of him. He was a great father—the best he knew how to be. All I could think about as I held his weak, frail hand was how much our hands looked the same. What an odd time to realize that I have hands like my father's. I thought to myself, "I am losing my dad, my Nonnie— he would want me to be strong, remember all he stood for, the things he taught me and to never forget him!" My heart was breaking. Yet through all of this, a few hours earlier one of my sisters told me a story about the great possibility that he was not my biological father. In that split second, I felt a bit of anger and disdain toward her but the feeling quickly faded. It faded so fast that I didn't even have time to look the part of an illegitimate child, I snapped right back, checked my feelings about the story and responded in the way any daughter who had been loved by her father would. "He is my ONLY Father!"

Needless to say, no story told can take his fatherhood away from my or his existence. It is here to stay.

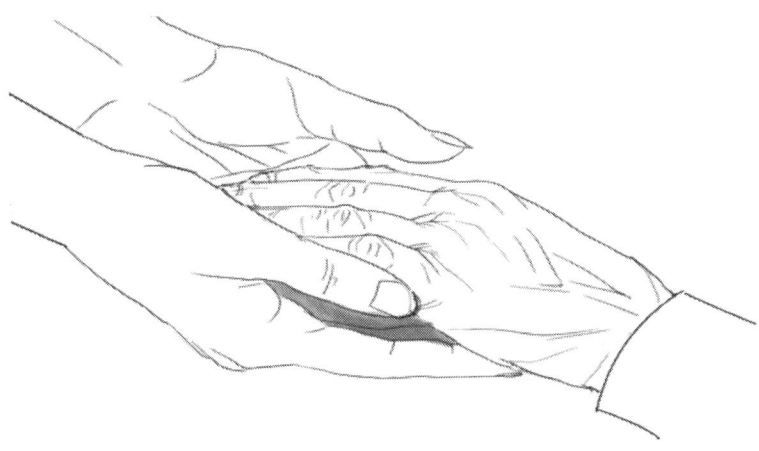

"Father"

Uncomfortable and so uneasy is what you seemed,

When you tried showing affection to anybody.

In your time Father, hugs only when a child was young,

The only time a man should hug his daughter or his son.

Now all grown and having my own way about me,

I am going to show you affection without shame

Do exactly the opposite of what you showed me.

I have vowed to always be affectionate.

The day has come and I don't care to ever stifle it,

As you lay here, me being told your time is near

I know this would be one of the times I need to show you that affection

Give you a hug and say "Father I love you" I am here holding your hand so have no fear.

If you were awake and able to speak, I know you would've said I love you too

I am also aware this way of showing affection would be new to you.

You taught me most of the things you felt I needed to know

I understand now you felt it was needed for me to grow

Inside and out molding and teaching me to be a woman

Father, thank you for not always feeling the need to hold my hand

Those hands patted our backs when we were in tears, made money to buy us clothes,

Clapped at our accomplishments but rarely used to hold us close.

You are that man Father, as I became older, those affections you did shun

I now use my hands to hold, hug, and kiss you on the cheek or forehead so you can feel my love, before your life is gone.

When that time comes no matter how sad I am,

I will always remember this moment as you lay here,

Doing for you what you did for me so many times, assuring me everything will be okay just by holding my hands.

When my father found out about what I had endured, I could see the pain, discomfort, and his confusion on his face. What do you do when someone you love is hurt by someone else you love? He was okay with the decision my sister Alice made, to demand he (the monster) never come to our home ever again. And so, it was! It didn't end there for me though, for some reason I was a target for many others.

CHAPTER 2

"Mammy"

There are so many phases a person who has been sexually abused can go through, especially when the appropriate help is not available. Of course, my conclusion or you can say my opinion, is based on my experience as a victim and a law enforcement officer, not a mental health professional. Some, if not most of those phases can be self-destructive. For example, it can lead to low self-esteem, being guarded and secretive, not trusting anyone, to promiscuous behavior, drug addiction, and sometimes suicide. Knowledge is power. That phrase has meaning beyond just *you knowing*, it also means that you can set yourself free and let it be known that you are a victim. It is bad enough when a child is molested but it makes things worse when they see things done by adults around them, which can lead to more confusion about intimacy.

"The Face"

Seemingly be, not of the standard held up to this confused society

Considered to be audacious in terms of gossiping mongers

Whether you were happily welcomed or not,

Or simply put it may not have been titled in any manner other than you are here and that's just that.

In great reverence don't ever forget where you came from!

No matter the circumstances, length of time it took.

Received the care or not to be received, others made it here through God's good graces, this I do believe

Loved by most in bare form, some denied or tossed away, some hop-ing we had gone back to where we came from.

Jarring, may have been or is, we came

Each breath, take time without second thought

Hard or little she fought

From her, life and through her canal is whence we came,

Life given, evidence, our existence, one way or another shall stay.

Of no importance now, she may or may not have held her head in shame.

Is or once was

You know not, look at; find in your mind the face;

Given guidance, solicited hugs, an ear,

Honesty, compassion, a sheltered lie here and there.

In heart, best interest you shall find.

Nurturing rendered, a lesson on faith, witnessing for you a prayer.

Whenever, Wherever, or Whomever,

Giving a whole or pieces, by nature to nurture.

Some memories just stick with you, seeing my mom at the sewing machine making outfits for me and my siblings. Today, when I'm invited to a party, I start thinking, it's time to go shopping for an outfit! Back then, because money was tight, my mom was always hustling up something on her sewing machine for us to wear just before we took a trip. It was so easy for her; she was very skilled at sewing! On this particular day, she dressed me up and took me on the bus ride with her. I was no older than three years old. Of course, I cannot remember the particulars of the bus ride but I do remember it was hot and sunny outside, and the following describes me waking up already at our destination.

"Dream"

I had ribbons in my hair, white knickers and a vest on to match,

Tears running down my cheeks

In this strange house and being alone, or so it seemed

Hearing the sound of her voice I woke from my sleep.

I expected her to come running to the sound of my weep.

Is this a dream?

Surely, my cry she did not hear

Or she would have jumped to my rescue with that motherly instinct and a small portion of fear.

No more than three-feet tall, of the bed I crawled.

Mammy where are you? I thought.

Following her voice through the strange house, with courage my fear I fought.

Hoping you would hear the sound of my feet as I walked slowly in search of you

Mammy please listen to hear the pitter-patter of my feet.

She is lost, I thought, please come to me

I thought it was a dream

Your voice behind the door, I could hear

On my tiptoes and through the keyhole I stared

I saw as you were lying on the bed

With a man, who was not my father, his chest cushioning your head.

Now all grown up, your past told to me

I came to realize, no it wasn't just a dream but a true part of your story.

It definitely was not a dream.

CHAPTER 3

Innocence Lost

I am not sure how long after this incident my mother left for America because I was so young. Eventually we became a family of twelve. My parents raised ten children together, and although while growing up we heard rumors and some stated facts that not all ten children were my father's, the majority of the time there was love and togetherness encouraged by both my mom and dad. Even my existence was rumored not to be a part of my father's doing. I can say for certain though, if that is true, I never cared because he was the only and greatest father to all of us and I will always cherish that. My mother too, I believe, gave her 100 percent, which is all any child can expect from their parents once they are old enough to comprehend and process how their parents were raised. I believe we cannot, expect something or anything from someone, which they do not have to give. We cannot go back and give our parents the knowledge nor the opportunities they struggled to afford us. Although some of what and how they did things, may be considered incomprehensible in this day and age. We can and should be forever grateful that we have the opportunity to decide upon what and how to utilize those things in the process of raising our own children. We can take and give what we deem to be good and leave the rest behind. I don't mean forget about it, I mean use it "those ways" to help us improve ourselves as a person and as parents—storing them in the "*don't give*" *or* "*give*" *to our children box*. It turned out this was the same man my sister was implying to be my biological father. Go figure!

"Speak when you are spoken to and answer when you are called." "Little girls should be seen and not heard." These were common phrases used by my older siblings when reprimanding the younger ones. To me, they all sounded like stated demands of oppressive slavery phrases passed on from generation to generation— Subservient. I would like to believe we as a society have a better understanding of why it is important for us to listen when children speak. They are people too! They have important things to say!

"Can You See My Fear?"

Look at me; can you see my fear

No, all you can see is my little head covered with braids consisting of my dark brown hair.

All you can see is the thought of the perverted pleasures you get when you force yourself upon me.

Look at my face half-brother, friend of my sisters, it is me this little innocent, not for long though, baby.

Someday to be a woman scarred into promiscuity and confusion, a woman never wanting to truly open herself to loving or trusting any man.

Stop! I beg of you! In my mind only, because you put your finger onto your lips, shushing me.

Look at me, do you see my fear? I am your daughter, your sister, your mother even.

Look at my face; no you can't because it is smothered into your waist.

The height of me barely reaching your knee,

You pulled; out it came, on my back by you I am placed.

If not for being so young, I surely would have prayed.

Your fingers, your size, the smell of what I know now to be alcohol on your breath during all of your overnight stays.

Can you see my fear?

No, for I am a baby filled with innocence and know not yet I need to be afraid.

Can you see my fear?

"How long did it go on for?" was the question. I was constantly in fear, not knowing whom or when would be the next time. I never even thought of speaking about it. There were no threatening words, I never told because I simply didn't realize I should. Too young to think of telling, residing with the fact that he was older, too young to think whether or not it was right or wrong, whether I should tell or not, just too young to give it any thought at all, but not too young to know it felt very uncomfortable. "Respect your elders." Respect your elders, now that's a tricky one, one that I not only imagine should be elaborated on but do know for a fact "It should be elaborated upon!"

"Listen"

I didn't know I should have said no or screamed when you laid me on the bed

Spreading my legs apart, placing your fingers then your head

I thought it was a secret only because you told me so

I had no idea these acts you did was something I should've told

You knew because of your experience touching me that way would make me feel pleasure

Introducing to me to a world of forbidden acts at the age of four or five

You knew I didn't know any better.

As I began to understand I felt so wrong for enjoying the ways in which I was touched

It took me years to overcome, to love myself again or to feel alive

It was so many of them I had no idea what was being done was wrong

A touch here pokes there, Dear God look at what they have done

Creating a sense of guilt in me, and leaving me with such low self-esteem

Confusing me about what I should or shouldn't feel so I acted out to extremes

By the age of six or seven I was trying to French kiss an older man who once visited

Thank God he was one with morals who sensed something was wrong

Showing no signs of being tempted and never was he interested.

Pulling back with fear in his eyes, disgusted with the action taken by this little child.

The devil's temptation, the offer I made he surely did deny

By the age of eight or nine I learned some were attracted to me and wanted what I should hold dear

They would touch, poke, and jab at me every time they came around,

I didn't try to stop them any longer; it was as though I didn't care.

Then that day came when at some point I felt it wasn't right

Each time they came around I would stay away or stand with others

But that only made them come at me when all were asleep late at night

I would squeeze my legs together and just as tight, shut my eyes

And ask for it to be a dream, for, all these touches I now despised

When daylight comes, they would speak to me as nothing ever happened

Mingle with the rest of the family, sit and eat at the same table

But me, never a word would I say, I wanted someone to look into my eyes and know my little soul was broken.

I wanted to be saved by anyone. Speak when you are spoken to, I have always been told

This is my time to speak; this little girl who learned she should be seen and not heard is slowly losing her little soul.

That night came and as he approached, I locked the door as I slept

In the room, my newborn nephew I held tightly as I wept

Hoping he would never be able to open the door, as he pried at the lock on his knees with that knife.

God knows best; he didn't get in, God saved my precious life.

Asleep, in terror and anxiety as deep as ever, I did fall

Then came daylight and with anger in their voices I did hear my name as they called

Opening the door with nothing but relief, now in my mind I hear

Little girl you have been seen and now need to be heard! Speak without your fear.

Speak when you are spoken to. I spoke and I answered as I was called

Why did you lock the door my girl? At last, permission to speak, and so I told it all.

CHAPTER 4

Angels

Here is a thought, you teach a child to tell a lie is wrong but when they are open enough to tell the truth, you call it being disrespectful. Do you want a lie or do you want the truth? Be ready for the truth if that is what you ask for.

As a child I didn't understand most of the things I did or why I did them, but as a mature adult I know now, I have been blessed to be placed by God in places to help me understand.

His name was David Samaad, and he worked in the fowl depot that was located at the bottom part of the two-story house my family lived in when I was a child. Dave was a very close family friend. It could have all gone so wrong—I couldn't have been any older than six or seven years old. He, "God" sends his angels to watch over us when we least expect it and sometimes, we know right then and there just as he does. Other times, it takes us time to process that it was God sending an Angel. That process time can be minutes, days or sometimes years. I was so young that the details of how or why were either not expressed to me or of no importance to me but I ended up at Dave's family's house, particularly in his room. It was a small room and I was on the floor playing while Dave laid on his bed trying to take a nap. Dave was much older than I; he was in the same age group as my eldest sister Jeneva or probably a bit older. He seemed to be a kind person and well-liked by my brothers and sisters. During his attempt to nap, I remember him turning his head toward me, but again, I have no memory of what he said before it happened. I leaned over to Dave and tried to kiss him the way grown-ups kiss. Dave looked at me in a way I had never seen him look at me before, he reached out to me with both hands and pulled me toward him in what seemed to be slow motion. He whispered to me gently with a look that took me into whatever trance he was in, he held me tight against his chest and said, "Don't ever do that again, that is not a nice thing that you just did. Where did you learn that from?" At that moment, I felt sad. I had no idea I was doing something wrong, I thought kissing him was normal and he would be receptive to it. "Thank God he wasn't!" As a mother, a victim of molestation and sexual abuse, I praise my God every day, sometimes I find myself just singing and thanking God with these words. These are the verses of my song that I sing to Him when I start remembering days filled with innocence and all the Dave Samaads of the world …

I thank you Lord, thank you Lord, thank you, thank you, thank you. Thank you, thank you, thank you, Lord.

I sing it over and over again, this way if there ever comes a day that I cannot sing it; He knows that I have always been thankful.

"Because of You?"

Every morning I awake I thank you

I give thanks for every breath I take

This journey I know has already been written, every decision I make.

Every thought I think, word I speak, and thing I do

It is all because of your generous mercies to me you show

Thank you, Lord,

Oh, you are my Savior

I am blessed to have you as my God

I stumble but I see because of you I never fall

Times get to be, oh so hard

Softened by my faith and belief in you, a new day comes and yesterdays become just yesterdays and suddenly today doesn't seem so bad

Because of you I never fall, you give me strength to forever stand tall

Thank you, Lord,

My Savior through it all, Thank you Lord

Your promises you have kept; To clothe and feed me as the fields, to spread your wings to be my shield, to give me hope and tender love.

You quench my thirst because I believe in your presence up above.

My needs are no more, this I want the world to know, if by chance I don't see tomorrow.

Thank you, Lord, Thank you, Lord

You are my Savior and I'm so blessed you are my God.

The one and only God, my Savior, forever my Savior, Thank you, Lord.

I have come to realize, not everyone receives that blessing of understanding God's great or sometimes small mercies. I had to be totally still in order to hear what God was and still is saying to me. Be still, listen, and follow his lead. There was a lot for me to hear, a lot for me to listen to, and an enormous amount for me to follow. I am still trying and my faith continues to mount, my deeds are becoming more wholesome and with that so is my patience and my being. I know now He wanted me to know that the good guy does exist. He was preparing me for my journey, instilling hope and belief by sending Dave Samaad to be that example, leaving me with the hope good people are out there. There is good and there is evil. *He* made sure through it all, that I never forgot.

Time passed and we moved to a new home not far from where we lived—but I never saw Dave Samaad again. I have asked about

Dave and told the story to some of my siblings, so they too can thank him every time they think of him. I heard that he is now disabled and in a wheelchair. I hope to see him one more time in my lifetime, so I can hold him as gently as he held me and whisper, "Thank you."

"Angels"

There are Angels all around

Some covert, some you can spot right away

They are spread out taking care of us all every day

Angels of specific support, Angels of encouragement,

Angels with big broad shoulders to lean on.

Some to guide us, if or when we go astray.

CHAPTER 5

The plea

I pray for better days, a continued decrease of victims and evildoers … **I am to know God is.**

"Help"

Before you act on your uncontrollable need to violate your victim

Stop and take a moment to think

Think of how wrong it is to do what you are about to and where it stems from within you

This act of violating another person in anyway, bringing shame to yourself, making them your prey

Is this what you really want to do?

Some say it's a disease and you can't control yourself

I, who once was a victim, don't believe it's true,

Others say, when you were a child someone must have done something, causing hurt to you.

Whatever the reason you think is giving you the urge to do what you do

You need to recognize something is so terribly wrong with the things you do.

Don't let that demon inside take you down

Once you commit that act there is no turning it around

Taking the innocence from someone special,

Destroying a life other than your own

There is nothing about that to be proud of at all

Inside there will be a seed of hate that will be sewn.

I imagine you've never spoken to anyone about the shameful things you do before

I also imagine that's because you get your urge, think about what you do and you make yourself sick right to your core.

You may think no one knows your secret because you've never told.

That hole in you that is so deep and dark, seeps through your pores

Stinks so badly, from afar some can sense your ugly soul.

There are things you say or sometimes do subconsciously

That catches people's attention and they view you suspiciously

There are people willing to help, people you can speak with

Reach for help before you act out, otherwise

Hell will come crashing down on you and you will later regret it

It would be better for your intended victim.

That's what he or she will be called "Victim" after your despicable act,

A harmed, injured, or killed person, why would you want to live with that?

Getting the help you need would be good for you most of all

You will be saving yourself from so much shame

In the eyes of those you love, to them you will never be looked at the same.

One of the so many things that will change in your life;

Your family and friends will surely cut you off.

Things will be made harder each day after, for you to simply attempt to strive.

Not to mention the person whose innocence you will take and violate

In whose mind for you there will always be hate,

Don't wait until you have committed the act that will change your life forever

Instead reach out to get some help; at least try and make yourself better.

I still hold on to some of the names from my stories because of love. Names held because the evildoers are no longer in existence and no one else needs to be hurt by their actions. The pain inflicted on me, stops here with me. It is a sacrifice made to not allow evil to gain strength. No regrets, none at all.

Wouldn't it be so wonderful if we could trust everyone we love?

My experiences have taught me there is good and there is evil.

Sometimes we can spot evil right away and sometimes we become prey. It is important to point it out to others when we see it, so the dark can come to light. It is a step in saving someone else from becoming another victim—Self-preservation.

"Who Can I Trust?"

Who can I trust?

Why can't I lay here and get some rest ?

and not have to worry about you acting out on your lust?

I am tired, you may not know,

My self-esteem and my will to be me is oh, so low.

Who can I trust?

As you put your hand between my legs

I want to snap my fingers and turn into dust.

Please show me God, Who can I trust?

"Don't Do This To Me"

Stop don't do this to me

I trust you can't you see

I look to you for everything I need

Don't do this to me please!

For the rest of my life I will have to take you with me

This heavy load you force upon me

In my sleep you will become my nightmares

No child should ever have to live in this type of fear.

When I speak you will be at the tip of my tongue

Hanging to my words and hoping I don't tell anyone

Most of my pain, if not all, will be caused by your perverse and dirty ways

There is no excuse for your lustful actions on your overnight stays.

Every touch and every feel and every smell you take has been unsanctioned

When I cry you will be in every drop of my tears

Please don't let yourself become my nightmares.

Stop don't do this to me!

My heart says I should love you

You are someone entrusted with my well-being

My soul says to discern you

You are the devil that only I can see

Especially when you do the things you do

Please stop touching me

Touching me in ways you aren't supposed to

Please don't do this to me!

CHAPTER 6

The talk

No regrets because without being told, I know family means everything. I know, how my siblings and I were raised affected each of us differently. I understand we are individuals and each of us must own up to our actions, simply put, "Own up to Them!" I have my memories and my sisters and brothers have theirs! Good and bad, we have them. My love for my family, both then and now, helps me to carry my own memories.

Sometimes people we love dearly, (family members or close friends) do things to us that are wrong and we find ourselves torn between the love we have for them and the pain they have caused us. I have learned not because we love someone, means they shouldn't have to suffer the consequences for the wrong they have done. As a victim our main concern, first and foremost, is how to *not be a victim*. Our hearts are sometimes softened by the love we have for the person who is doing the wrong to us. The truth is, if they love us half as much as we love them, they would not harm and victimize us. We must love ourselves more and know that we deserve better from that person, be it a father, mother, brother, uncle, stepbrother, sister's boyfriend, teacher, and so on. Our healing only starts when we stand up for ourselves, and yes, standing up is the beginning of your freedom from victimization. *Tell it all.*

"The Truth"

The touch on the chest that makes you uncomfortable.

That happened when everyone left the dinner table.

The touch on the leg some nights

For some reason that touch didn't feel right

The hand on your head or the touch of your hair

That comes along with that uncomfortable look or stare

The discomfort when they come around

All those times you pray for them to leave town

The confusion this person makes you feel

Every time backs are turned, one more touch they would steal

The secrets they say are precious and between the two of you

Don't believe for a moment that this is true.

The peeks they take while you are in the shower or the tub,

Sometimes asking you to give them a kiss on the lip or a weird back rub

Daddy, stepfather, aunt, uncle, cousin, Neighbor;

Asking you to do things you somehow feel you aren't supposed to.

Mother, stepmom, friends of your parents, Brother, sister, Teacher, babysitter;

Touching on your private parts and having you touch them there too.

Yes, this can happen even when it's someone you love and trust.

Tell the truth about what happens, because for it to stop, you must.

Tell it to all who will listen, tell it to the whole wide world!

Keeping that dirty little secret is not good for you to hold. Remember if you really want help tell only the truth.

Like most very young girls who lose their virginity, I was put to shame, sentenced, and condemned. I now know, I am human, made in his image; one of God's children despite the fact, at times I was lead to thinking there was "no hope" for me. "I am and have always been full of hope."

My question was not, "why did they treat me the way they did?" I knew I could not control their behavior I could only control my own but, "why did I do some of the things I did"? The answer eluded me and as a result it left me feeling less than good, less than what society considers proper, it left me feeling like garbage. At that time, I felt I was a good person, fighting to show them I was not "garbage" and I would not always be seen as garbage — "someday they will see the real me". I have grown and so have they.

"Don't Judge Me"

I lay down for words

Not of my own lust

I lay down for looks of perversion

A sweet talk here and there

For me no satisfaction gained

For them only

I open myself to evil spirits as I lay

Teach me don't judge me

When I walk in a provocative way

Don't call me a whore

I don't feel any wrong each time I lay on my back

Ask me questions; get the information you need to teach me

This way about me is none other than promiscuity

Heaved upon me by the men who came at me in stacks

They have spread my legs open time and time again

Probing and prodding; shushing and scheming before I was ten

Don't judge me, save me

Teach me how precious I am

Teach me how precious it is

So precious they stole it when no one was looking

All those sinful men

Stole my precious virginity

Don't judge me, teach me

With all that has happened, try to save me

Teach me that with all that, still I am.

The weird thing is I never asked myself when it would end. It—meaning the sexual abuse, physical abuse and the promiscuity. If I had known it was wrong, I imagine, I would have prayed for it to end. Then one day it all just stopped. All in God's time—I have learned—All in God's time. When God said it was time... IT stopped... I was able to breathe and let it out. It took a lot of hard losses as well as a lot of beautiful gains before I realized it was all a part of God's plan, no one else's not even mine.

"Don't be afraid"

You have the ability to speak, so talk

Raise your head because that is how your body is structured

Your head sits on your body upright

Don't be afraid, stand up and face up to the fight

Mankind made fear and shame.

He created manipulation and intimidation but you should know to me, it is all but a game.

His words he uses to hurt you

Into his world of scheme and betrayal, oh what a tainted view.

Don't be afraid, open your mouth

Speak, yell, and talk about it because this is your only way out.

Out of this man-made creation, this physically, verbally or emotionally abusive corner called hell.

Shout it out, this abuse to you he will no longer sell.

Don't be afraid, talk about it

Stand up for yourself; take back what was given to you.

Own it, it is yours the right to speak, smile, feel safe, to be loved, to love; these are the things you are rightfully due.

Say it as surety and let it be known

Living in this world of molestation and abuse, you will no longer own.

Bring it to light let everyone see, dragging it in sight is the key to setting you free.

CHAPTER 7

My right to feel safe and to exist as I am.

My comfort level does not dictate the comfort level of those around me, and it is important for us to listen when a person says, "They make me uncomfortable." How can you trust someone when they don't listen to how you feel? Be a "trusted outlet ... Listen."

I am happy to be here to tell my stories. I find it to be therapeutic. The memories never go away, but when the abuse is committed by multiple people as it did to me and the victim is as young as I was, there is often confusion as to who did what and when. It is very disheartening for me to be in a position where I remember the incident taking place. I was half-asleep and there was a conversation taking place while the act was being committed. I heard their voices but because I was so traumatized by the ordeal, I was not sure who committed the act. They were all close family members. At first, I felt apologetic, fear of calling the wrong name but now after living and thinking about it, I realize there is absolutely no need for me to apologize to anyone for my victimization.

No spirit of hate, only spirit of release and healing. My writing is part of my support system.

"Fight"

The heat in my body
The pitted feeling in my belly
I don't know if I exhaled or inhaled last
My pulse is beating so fast and my knees are weak
I can't breathe, stay calm is what my brain tells me, stay calm

Can't swallow, my eyes are watery

Hands are up, Pray and beg is what I should do

But I can't speak

Ten minutes it seems, too long however the length of time,

Too long, ten to fifteen seconds truly

Fear takes over, faded visions I see

Stay calm or fight, what should I do?

As my life flashes before me,

I fight or I fought, did I stay calm?

I begged, I can't or I did beg, or so I thought

Crushing, no choking, yes crushing and choking

I can't breathe, how long before…

I need to breathe, fight, I see darkness in my sight

Flash of death, I want to live,

I ask myself is it too late, is it too late to fight

Fight for my life

Digging into the pit of what is in front of me,

Your empty eyes

I want to live God, so in my mind I prayed

You are choking me out, out of my life

I fought for this life you didn't appreciate

I will keep fighting, I am no longer afraid

I want to live.

"Endless"

I am not sure when it was you became an important part of my soul

I do know you are here today and I am so sure you will be here if I live to grow old.

I see you in everything I am privileged to see, I feel you in everything someone does for and with me

Your presence exists in every breath I take

And more so every morning I awake.

Your mercies some small as a grain of salt

My graciousness to you every day I shall exalt.

Through you I see eternity, through me the effervescence of your existence shines undoubtedly.

The warm burning sensation I feel in my stomach each time I think of all you have created and all you have done

Tells me this story has only just begun.

For, time is endless we all know, my name in your book before there was any other trace.

I imagine in your book full of names there exists not a sight of space.

As I use this time from you I graciously borrowed,

I try desperately to live my life on the straight and narrow.

This righteous road made to follow as lonely as it seems

I look forward to your and my togetherness to the fullest extreme

All of those promised tomorrows that you have in store for me.

Your love, I feel, can only be described as sovereign and endlessly ...

Not knowing any better about the consequences, I had consensual sex for the first time when I was fifteen but was much younger when I lost everything that was supposed to be held so dearly with my virginity. Now after all these years, with the knowledge and wisdom bestowed upon me through trials and tribulations, both welcomed and unwelcomed, I ask myself why I gave away my treasures at such a young age? Why am I called, a "whore" by the people I love? Through life's lessons and as a result of my work experience in interviewing and investigating, I can now answer without hesitation, without shame or fear; but with self-understanding; much higher self-esteem and with the graciousness of having defeated condemnation; I answer ... "I had no idea how precious my body, me, my vagina was! I gave it to almost anyone that hinted to me they wanted it, instead of being forced and having it taken, which would then leave me feeling violated and with a lack of control over my own body.

Especially after being groped and poked by some of the men that came into arms-length of me. I was tired of being groped and poked! I had no idea when I did give it away, I should have at least had some understanding of what it meant and what it is capable of producing. I one day came to realize, what I was doing gave me a "false" sense of me having control, instead of me showing resistance and then being forced to have sexual intercourse. I once watched an episode of the Oprah Winfrey show many, many, years ago and the message was on saying "NO." We should practice saying the word "NO" so it gets easier. This has really worked for me! I walked around my apartment repeating the word "No" over and over again because I felt I was living proof of one of those persons she spoke of that found it hard to say "NO." I am living proof that repeatedly saying "No" out loud works. Unfortunately, not everyone listens and accepts the word NO" but more importantly what I learned is, how you say it can give it even more meaning. "No" has gotten me out of some very uncom-fortable and unwanted situations. Thank you, Oprah Winfrey!

"No!"

If you don't mean it, don't say it.

When you do say it, say it like you mean it.

Let your body language say it too,

Saying it with your mouth and with the right body language can certainly save you.

Don't say it with a smile or low as though you are not sure.

Say it loud and with a serious face, then run out the door!

When it is said in any other way than serious

It puts you in a bad position and also that's not good for any one of us.

Be it when your date violently demands that you get in the car

Or if sexually, you feel it is being taken too far.

As soon as you feel that unwanted discomfort,

Don't ever second-guess that feeling of fear in your gut.

Allow your first instinct to guide you home

Otherwise you may find yourself in danger and alone.

Scream "No" as loud as you possibly can.

It doesn't matter where you are,

That scream of "No" may just crush their vicious plan.

Any caring person would understand

Even if later you found you may have made a mistake

Were afraid and so uncomfortable you felt at that moment your life was at stake!

Scream as loud as you can don't think twice.

If it doesn't feel right ... Yell, NO!

Saying "No" like you mean it can be used as a lifesaving device.

YOU CAN'T DO THIS...

NO!!!

DON'T DO IT...

STOP IT···

The trauma a person goes through can only be understood when it is you. Patience, love, a listening ear from those around you—the victim of the sexual abuse, can be very helpful. There are those of us who want to talk and need to talk about it, and there are those who are ashamed and stay silent. For me, I felt as though the more I let the words out the cleaner I became, telling took their dirty out and off of me and sent it right back to them. Go figure, now they are the prey and I am the hunter.

"Hanging on my every word, holding their breath with everything I would say.

Hoping their story wasn't the one I would tell that day—Karma."

There are so many forms of trust. So many ways a person can be victimized. What I understand from my experiences with trust is, to be a person who is considered to have a trustworthy character is a blessing. On the other hand, to be considered a person who cannot be trusted can lead to a life empty of love. To be empty of love is to me, to be soul-less.

For all the young men and women who have been told all the nice things they wanted to hear and given the pretty and expensive gifts they dreamt of, or for those of you who are feeling like the ugly duckling and were or are not part of the in-crowd, before you give your most valuable assets away, your magic, for mere nice words and pretty things; know that you are worth much more! *You are beautiful in the eyes of all who love you.* Liking, loving, respecting, and trusting in yourself is where *awesomeness* begins. If you do not like, love, respect, and trust in yourself, then how can you expect anyone to like, love, respect, and trust you!

"Kiss and Tell"

Do you really want to, kiss and tell, I open my box of treasures for all your sweet talk, telling me what you think I want to hear, for your charm I fell.

Should you really want to kiss and tell?

Tell that you had me, maybe that you took my virginity ... sharing what's supposed to be our privacy to all your homeboys because of your insecurity.

Once I allowed you in, you should have shown the utmost respect to me.

I gave you a taste of a precious piece of what is inside of me.

So disrespectful and undeserving you are, now I am forced to tell your true story.

Coming to my crib with your two hands swinging empty, which means shame on me because I gave my preciousness to you for free.

You didn't even have the stamina to hang with me.

No foreplay, just panting like a dog and bang, bang it was.

A shut out after one-two-three.

Snoring so hard as though you traveled a real lover-man's journey.

Hmm ... go ahead kiss and go tell so that I can tell the whole story.

Truth; My story can make you big or small, thin, fat, short, or tall.

Ruin your self-confidence for the rest of your life,

just by saying you couldn't get me to climb over the wall.

Go ahead I dare you to kiss and tell.

My story; Such a big disappointment!

My little hands swallowed your little it, at your most exciting moment.

Do you really want to kiss and tell?

You only feel as big a man as I want you to feel.

My words my groans and my movements are what makes you beat your chest.

One of these words, "small," "limp," or quick and your manhood I shall steal.

Do you really want to kiss and tell?

Better you should have known, how dare you think you were in control and really, I am the one with the real storybook key.

Do you really want to kiss and tell, Boy?

Or are you a man who is going to respect our privacy?

I simply had no *idea*! Yes, of course my mother told me that having unprotected sex was not a good idea, but that was years after it had been forcefully taken and weeks after I had already consented. When at fifteen I asked permission to get birth control pills, her suspicions were right, and what she said was "I hope you are not full of fuck!"

It took me about thirty seconds to understand what she meant by that, after all, the next thing she said was "The last thing you need to do is get pregnant." It took bad experiences in my life, to understand years later, why "The last thing I needed to do, was get pregnant."

She gave me permission to get the birth control pills and while I was at the Clinic I was told by the doctor, "The horse is already in the gate".

"What does that mean?" I asked.

"You are already pregnant."

I was terrified, sick to my stomach, confused, afraid, and most of all, feeling so alone!

He dumped me four months later!

"Here Tomorrow"

I know what it is like to feel alone in the world

So many people around me

Yet here I am drained by negativity,

Walking around like a lost soul.

Feeling self-destructive and not understanding why I feel that empty hole

Sometimes thinking I don't belong in this world

Thinking of what a good and kind person I am,

Feeling as though I am the only one that gives a damn

Getting lost in that whirlwind of sorrow

Wondering why would I want to meet any tomorrows

Feeling understood was so important to me

And that was my worst thought, because this thought almost destroyed me.

Then one day filled with all of the frustration

A light switch went on with brilliance like the maker of light, Con Edison

In that light I saw, this whole world is made up of variety

And my breath, is not based on who understands me

I am here to give the world my different, I now see

To add some of me into this big and challenged society

To be that someone I was sent to be, to be the one here to understand when I meet another like me.

To give them hope that they are not alone

To help share what is in that misunderstood, soon to be understood, zone

It is all, important to the world you see

To share that different you with this learning and growing society

There is enough space for us all to fit in

Even if, there comes a time another type of misunderstood should show up again.

Not wanting to meet tomorrow, I must tell you, really is not an option

Especially for folks like us, who are where we are, filled with misunderstood emotions.

Okay, to them we are misunderstood

I now understand I am a part of a different brotherhood

For we are all humans and aren't supposed to know it all

So I now wear my shirt of "Misunderstood" alive and standing tall

This society needs us to be a part of the variety

So when tomorrow comes you wear "your" misunderstood shirt

It will make you feel better, try you will see.

Then look at yourself in the mirror and say, this society needs this "Misunderstood Me!"

It became so tiring, I learned by force to be very tolerant. I do understand myself better today than years ago, even yesterday. I love the person I am. I am that person who I needed when I was a little girl, someone I could trust. I say this with great pride, humility, and grace. I know I am not perfect and what I have also come to know is—I AM not going to let my imperfections be an excuse to not try to be perfect.

I LOVE AND APPRECIATE ME

"Believe"

I thought it was wrong to feel sexual

What you did to me as a child caused me to put up a wall

A wall avoiding me to enjoy the very things my God created me with in order to love living and to care for all

My self-existence, is what you almost took away

By violating me mentally and physically, your stench on me cannot stay

The natural feeling of being sensual I thought was bad

But I know now those feelings I feel are proper but what you did makes me sad

I realize in this life I have to be able to love someone enough to give them my promise and my soul

Lay with them and trust that the wonderful life God has for me will now unfold.

To feel sexy and attractive is part of my womanhood

You tried to ruin me; you did what you did just because you could

I met someone and I was told he could make me whole again

He can restore me because what you did was your evil choice and not a part of his plan

He showed me how to feel good within myself once more

And explained to me, that you are a monster and rotten straight to your core

He said there is a big chance that one day you will come to him also

But although he is merciful your wrongdoings to others and me, he will never let it go

I trust him; since I've known him, he has never hurt or lied to me

He has once again made me whole, clean and now because of him I feel womanly and worthy

I can now be touched and touch another and not think or feel those touches are dirty

I know if he does, then everyone else can love me.

He said, "Believe." I said, "I do," and now of you, that monster, I am set free.

CHAPTER 8

The cycles

I Am one of your chosen vessels, Lord! I now take the time you have bestowed upon me to give testimony of your guided ways. God guided me to self-preservation, forgiveness, self-worthiness and gave me strength toward my healing. He heard my cry.

Abuse comes in many different forms and most of us have experienced it in one form or another. Some of us recognize it, yet to some, being treated that way is normal because they grew up seeing it happen in their homes every day. Abuse can be physical, mental, or verbal and it is never a healthy environment. I AM one of God's children. He said he will never forsake me.

"One Too Many"

It came so sudden out of nowhere,

So sudden I should have felt pain but I was so in shock and instead started to feel fear.

All I said was no and there it was

Your fist, it hit my face without any just cause

I see this on TV and have also read about it

But never had I thought I'd be a part of this shit

You kicked me as I lay on the floor in fear, I was so afraid

I had no time to react to what was happening; you are the one I had hoped if ever this would happen to me, you would come to my aid

All I kept thinking was "This is the man I love"

As you kept kicking and punching I saw no compassion as I looked at your face above

I was so shocked I couldn't even scream

As you kicked and punched me, shattering my dream

When I opened my mouth to ask you why

You punched me while holding my neck with your hands so tight

At that moment it dawned on me

No matter what your excuse for this behavior

This violent act is already one too many

I felt myself fading out,

When you put your lips onto my mouth

You said Baby I am sorry but I told you not to shout

With that I looked at you and said nothing else,

You pulled me up from the floor and told me go clean up myself

I trembled as I slowly walked away

Knowing after this with you I can't have you stay

If another day of this were to occur

I will not be in shock then, of that I am sure

Before I end my life by allowing you to abuse me this way,

911 as soon as I get the chance, this precious life will live to see better days.

Sometimes the element of surprise that occurs with the initial physical abuse can cause weakness and shock. It has been said, most times abuse is used to create fear and intimidation when the abuser is experiencing insecurity in their own short-comings or when they are losing that false sense of control, they think they need to have over another person—It's Not Love ...

"Chimes"

I am the woman who loved you enough to bear your children

Before they came into this world we were together starting as best friends

Together we dreamt of being with each other in good and bad times

We even talked about having a home and hanging musical chimes

Our imagination took us through the steps of our goals

Hoping as time passes, we'd be together as we grow old

Sharing even bathroom space, cold viruses, and Pamper changes together

Not imagining a hesitation in sharing anything with one another

Eating from the same plate, kissing each other while in the first morning breath stage.

Now living together as a family with our children

I sit and reflect on our togetherness back then

Oh, how we thought our dreams would come through

It comforted me to know I would be taking this journey standing right next to you

Now almost in the blink of an eye

Time has passed and I am forced to watch my dream as a family with you die

I wish I knew what you were thinking at that moment

Until that moment I had no doubt that our unity was God sent

The look in your eyes was so, I knew I had never seen

Calling me demeaning names, and acting in a way I would have never imagined

Taking me back to things you said to me, referring to me as your beautiful queen

Looking at the fear your actions placed into the eyes of our babies

Again, from you this was something I had never seen

Your hand was raised as though to hit me, your hesitation led to you pushing me

My innermost being, down to my soul, saw our disastrous journey's end start to unfold.

Now I am left to wonder, "What's next?"

Is he now going to punch me in the chest?

Made promises to each other, to the other we would never be unkind.

Now the kids have come and the only chimes I hear

Are notions from you, showing with your actions how little you now care

My heart's love for you still will never fade

But I saw your outburst made our children so afraid,

Now in my heart alongside the love I feel, you have placed a portion of fear

Fear enough to say, I now know I don't want you so near.

I went from one bad relationship to hoping the other one would be better. He was more mature, more responsible but too old for my parents to be comfortable. I was now seventeen with a baby and her absent father. I met someone new! I lied to him out of shame, I told him I was nineteen. I saw a glimmer of hope for a moment. He was better, but twelve years my senior and that made my parents scared. Scared I would be, in my Mom's term, "full of fuck". Meaning, get pregnant once again. So, they sent me away. I was heart-broken because he was very caring and respectful toward me. I had no choice in the matter so I kept it moving. I hoped to get it together for my and the sake of my baby. I respected their wishes and trusted in their guidance. Turned out, it was the worst decision that could've been made. I needed them more than ever at that time, as dysfunctional and as toxic as their relationship had become. I needed to be home.

Today, I believe in trusting my instincts especially when I experience uncomfortable feelings from men. Some think I am an expert at reading people because of my past profession as a law enforcement officer. I know, however, that it comes from my past experiences of being victimized. I will capture a giveaway look or sense of perversion from men with less than good intentions, which leads me to start a conversation to read their body language, and yes, reading body language was enhanced by my profession but also from years of being a victim of molestation. As a result of this gift, I am rarely ever wrong. It is so important to pay attention to some of the telltale signs.

"It Is Not Love"

When they tell you, I love you and I don't want you to speak to any one else but me.

If they see someone walking across the street look at you and they get angry

If they slap you in the face when you tell them you don't want to go

If they pull you by the neck, arm, or hair when you say no

Control and intimidation is what they hope to gain

If you stay that person will cause you pain

It's not Love

If they get angry when you say you will be okay making it home alone

When you get home they're outside your house and demanding to check your phone.

After they take your phone and check your calls

Their excuse is they love you so much it is driving them up a wall

Scheming their way out of what you may see in them

If you stay in this relationship it would really be a shame

It's not Love

When they tell you what you can and cannot wear

Then they say if you leave them, they will kill you, now they are instilling fear

They take your money and budget your daily spending

You leave work and you'd better be home early

It's not Love

If you feel intimidated by their yelling

When you feel afraid to tell them what you're feeling

They make you feel in danger when they don't get their way

If they demonstrate insecurity when you say go on ahead, I'd like to stay

When they accuse you of sleeping around with anyone you have a conversation with; If they haven't yet done so, this could be the first time you may take a hit

When they say, baby I am sorry I won't hit you again

Then say I love you so much and don't want you to have other friends

Hope will make you want to stay

And the affection you have for them, they hope will get them thier way

It's not Love

When they don't want you to go anywhere without them at your side

They call your job to check up on you every hour on the hour, there's no place now to hide

When they say if I can't have you, no one else will

Now they are actually contemplating the when and how they are going to make their kill

They have no problem doing it if they have no problem saying it, they can now envision the act of killing you

You now fear what he said will really come through

These are some of the signs that will take place

So be on point and keep this checklist in your intimate space

Don't let the next victim be you!

It's not Love.

CHAPTER 9

It's not over!

What is amazing is, we human beings, when conditioned to act a certain way from childhood, that performance becomes somewhat innate, it becomes a part of our instinct to survive and so we respond. I responded as though I was in control, in control of myself and what was happening to me.

At the time, in my young age (seventeen years old) looking at him, I thought he was probably about sixty-five years old. Now that I am older, I realize young people always think grown-ups are old, so if I had to guess he must have been around fifty years old, approximately six feet tall, Caucasian, with salt and pepper hair. I don't recall noticing the color of his eyes and yes, I had seen him before, even said hello a few times. He was a maintenance worker but he appeared harmless, he never showed any signs of perversion, always respectful. So, when he rang the doorbell and I looked out the window and saw it was him, I thought nothing of it. I opened the door and we started chatting as I sat on the stairs in the entryway. Embarrassment along with condescending judgmental statements kept me from telling anyone—especially since I was such a big disappointment to everyone by having a child at such a young age (sixteen years old). This was my "second chance to be a good person", why would I tarnish that second chance by saying, "Yes, I did open the door," "Yes, I did let him in." Oh, and by the way, "Yes I did fight with every ounce of strength I had in me!" "Yes, I did, not just say NO but SCREAMED, Stop It!" In the end all that mattered was that I was able to get up, dust myself off and keep moving. I sometimes wonder if there ever comes a time in their lives when they feel the need to confess their sins. Thereafter, began the stint of my promiscuity.

"Time"

Where is my fear to face the world?

In my throat, but I have none, by some I have been told

A smile in my words worn on my mask

To make these decisions, my courage to find is such a task

I wake not knowing where to or from

Focused, the aura I spring, for tomorrow I know must come

Footprints to follow, from those treasured in my space

I dare not fumble or show this fear on my face

My nerves are so stimulated by all that comes at me

That I must shake, I shall be labeled weak if anyone can see

I dare not look down, hesitate or shed a tear

No time for weak links, those are the rules that have been made clear

Second chances come so few and in between

Must get it right this time so to leave my slate clean

The world is tough but not as tough as I

I live this life, working hard to make it mine

Knowing the day will come, when I must leave it all behind

When it does, I will find my fear for then, I will know

I eventually ran out of precious time.

In the early 1990s, I was offered a job with an attorney as his assistant. I was so happy to accept because I saw it as a great opportunity to enhance my skills as a paralegal. On day three, I sat at my stenotype machine ready to take notes while he was dictating, and he noticed a run in my pantyhose. His remark to me was, "I would love to be that run in your pantyhose to see where it leads." I maintained my composure until the workday ended. I played the words over and over in my head while considering that we were in his office alone. It was very uncomfortable. I questioned the fear I felt and somehow convinced myself I was overreacting. I finished off the workday and never went back. If seeing a run in my pantyhose that I hadn't noticed took his thoughts there, I knew I would never be safe. You must always trust your instincts!

"The Prey"

I Remember

The brush against, not just once

The provocative remarks about my pantyhose that had a run

The offer to have drinks, your intimate share of thoughts

Your vile perverse looks, you disgust me

And no, with you, I don't ever want to do lunch

I shun you; try to keep my distance from you

Stay away from your office, make sure we are not together alone in the same place.

No, I Don't want to, I definitely don't want you or your unwanted advances

I don't want to answer but there is a need in me to keep my job

Questions about my personal life, as you ask them

Subjecting myself to your condescending tone and embarrassment

I involuntarily give answers and my distrust in you makes me somewhat of a snub.

Your promises of my promotion

Your compliments of my work

The carrot you dangle in front of me

All scheme and intimidation to have me as your personal clerk

So you can be near me, you are such a manipulative and deviant jerk

The guarded way you portray for me against everyone else

The conniving sense you create, trying to make me believe

In this environment I won't be able to take care of myself

Your unwelcomed, covert advances

That makes it hard for me to come to work each day

Because I feel as though I am working in hell

I will always remember

Sexual harassment, hostile working environment

Abuse of authority, a predator is what this all spells.

You remember all of it, don't you?

Me too, I remember!

Most of the people I allow into my space believe I am so strong. When they tell me this, my mind returns to all I have overcome. Sometimes in that moment I go there, and yes, I want to curl up and cry. I want to, for just "one moment" not be so strong. I understand I had to demonstrate a strong character because most of my life, people have taken advantage of me and now when I realize what is happening, I go into *warrior mode*—and I put on my armor of Prayer!

"I Am"

I strive every day to be okay!

I am as good as I am going to be.

And this is better than any of you may ever see

Understanding myself and why I feel the way I feel

Tells me how important it is for me to keep it real

I know where I've been and how I got to where I am

And with God's help I get to enjoy being free and taking this stand!

I have the right to tell my story without being judged

You look at me with envy sometimes scorn as though you are without a smudge

I walk with my head up high and speak aggressively

For in my mind no longer will I allow anyone to take advantage of me

I know who I am and what I should and shouldn't say

I take with me all the pain you placed upon me and in this book I shall let it lay

No longer running from my thoughts of you, for in this book it is you I cast away.

It is my duty to myself, my loved ones, and God to you I say

I will continue to strive at being good everyday!

I am as good as I can be today but tomorrow I will be better just you wait and see.

Tomorrow I will be always as good as I am to be.

Many of you have probably heard the saying "When in doubt leave it out!" Sometimes we are at a loss for words, especially when someone is grieving, experiencing a life-altering situation, or are simply going through a rough period. When that happens don't fight to find the "right" words, instead offering a hug or a soothing touch can go a long way.

"Words"

It can't ever be taken back

Especially when it is given from the heart

Sometimes it is given in such a wonderful manner

The way it is given, from experience, will always come to matter

Using it spitefully

Will be cause for it to be taken painfully

Before you use them always think about the message you would like to send

Especially when in a sticky situation and you are dealing with family or friends

The first few, you give to a person you've met for the first time

Can sometimes leave an impression of whether you are inconsiderate or kind

And yet, they can also be used to change the interpretation of things once ingrained in someone else's mind.

Using it can cause enough pain to scar someone for or out of life

Think before you do, otherwise with it comes acknowledgment of who said what to who

When talked about it can either lift you or cut your character down as with a knife

When used out of context a person can look very ignorant and not even realize

So be careful when you use them, familiarizing yourself before you use them, would be wise

The use of them can either make or break your very existence

They are magical like that

Sticks and stones may break things but words will never hurt you,

To me, makes absolutely no sense

Especially if you used them to tell a lie, hurt someone's feelings in the past or present tense

The bad karma it will bring shall rise and come out of the speaker's pores

They truly are magic

If given to a child in an appropriate manner, or someone yearning to have one day out of many, filled with laughter

It can save a life or be the maker of one of tomorrow's scholars

Use them considerably and wisely because to the ear, to the heart, and then air, they can't ever be taken back.

KILL YOURSELF!

YOU CAN DO IT! I HATE YOU!!

YOU MAKE ME SICK

YOU'RE SO UGLY! I AM HERE IF YOU NEED TO TALK!

YOU ARE THE LIGHT OF MY LIFE

YOU ARE THE BEST! I MISS YOU!

HAVE A WONDERFUL DAY! YOU SHOULD JUST GIVE UP!

I LOVE YOU I DON'T HAVE TIME FOR THAT RIGHT NOW!

LEAVE ME ALONE! **DO YOUR BEST!**

Nothing lasts forever; there is a season for everything. According to my father, "Even the longest prayer has an Amen." No matter how bad things get, you hold onto hope it will get better. Allow that hope (positive energy) to guide you on how the better is going to come. Always remember, the only way to go when you hit bottom is UP. Hope is faith, faith is God. In order to make it UP you must remove the things weighing you down to the bottom; wipe your slate clean!

"Forgiveness"

To all who have wronged me in any possible way

I give you my forgiveness for your actions

So, let not the thought of your wrong to me bring you any more trouble from this day.

My forgiveness to you is what I now offer.

Like a cup of your favorite hot tea with two scoops of sugar

Whether you meant your wrong or it was not intentional

It is time for me to let it be known I forgive you of it all

Some of the wrongs I have already forgotten

And some of them stayed with me because they were so rotten

Understand to forgive is not always to forget

Also, I am human and if it is, I haven't gotten there yet

Just as well, I need the forgiveness of all whom I did hurt

I know I've done my wrongs causing others pain

Whether they were intentional or not I must wear my own shirt.

I think back often trying to remember all the pain I have inflicted on others

Hoping I can find them now to apologize, if not then I pray

These words find them and they find me worthy of their forgiveness on this day.

If ever I said or did anything to cause you pain,

Whether it was intentional or not I am sorry and will try my best not to do it again.

I hope for you, not to take the burden of what I did to hurt you any further

As I now know, we are in control of what we do to each other

Giving and getting forgiveness I have come to learn

It is not something that is necessarily earned

It is something that can be offered by anyone who wishes to give it

And the recipient is usually burdened by shame and their guilt

When you forgive someone for doing something wrong to you

It forces you to stop dwelling on the wrong that had been done and gives you new energy to see the rest of your journey through

Even if you don't mean it wholeheartedly when you first say it

Because you said, "I forgive you," those words alone will be your guidance in seeing you through.

Offering a sense to them starting anew

Like each time you ask the maker, God, and He shows forgiveness to you.

Until you have walked in my shoes it would be sinful for you to utter a sound in the way of continued victimization. My shoes molded to the form of my feet as they took me through my journey, not yours. I forgive you …

CHAPTER 10

The Missing

When I look back, I don't see a mother and her child, I see a child and her youngen trying to reach the mountaintop, with no water to sustain them through their journey, no piton and no rope. Belief, hope, and an abundance of naiveté meant a journey of pain, deceit, loss, and perseverance.

Nothing can provide enough satisfaction when a loved one is violently taken from you. There is no closure. Your faith carries you through for the rest of your life. You never stop grieving. You are left learning to accept, and as time goes on you make adjustments in your grieving process in order to continue. No, it does not get easier, the pain does not go away, punishment or justice does not ease the pain, and you cannot turn the clock back. The pain stops when you stop. The key to surviving it is acceptance.

I came out of it alive but sadly alone, not without help of course. It was costly; life shaking and life changing. We are now free.

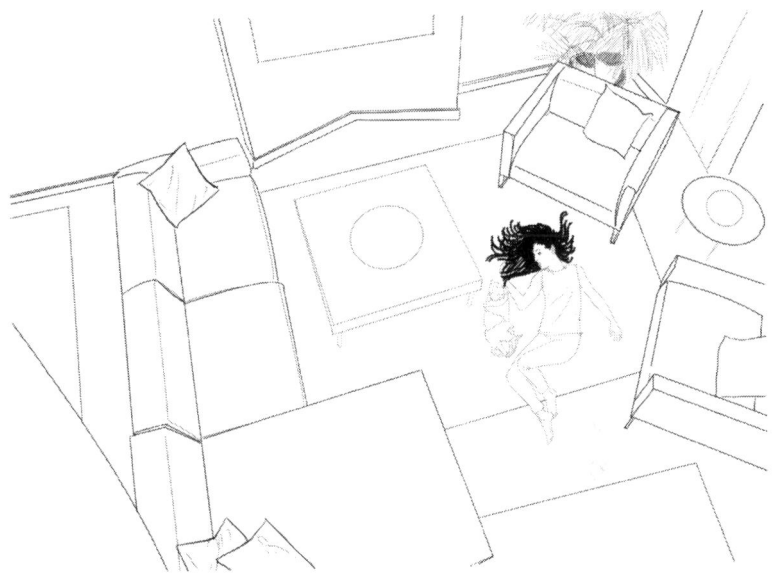

"Stained Soul"

I am not forgotten. I shall never be forgotten

Years shall go by, new bloodlines of generations shall come

Yet I will not be forgotten

Always remembered, my name shall be said, written and thought of, make no mistake I am remembered with Love.

Hidden outside the box is the truth to the circumstance of my loss

The ugly but so true a circumstance,

The whole truth, the real story of the injustice you did to me.

The look the other-wayers, the bystanders, spectators, the skin color haters.

Instigators and the nothing-doers,

The Sinners, even the hypocrisy bearers shall have their own, though not anything like yours.

That burden, of your intentional injustice.

You shall remember who I am. I will never be forgotten.

You shall remember me in a way no one else shall have to.

I shall be the face you see when there is no picture, the face you see when you look in the mirror.

The face you will see when the lids of your eyes are shut together, Through any good graces bestowed during your existence, going forward it shall be shattered by the memory of me.

You, the taker of my life, will never forget, I am all you shall see.

The presence of your existence shall speak my name when your mouth is not opened.

You shall forever carry the burden of my life being innocently taken.

This life that was lost, truth of murder yet to be told.

The loss of the life you stole has forever now stained your soul.

I will be with you always. I will never be forgotten,

You will always see my face, in your mind I stand like a picture in a frame.

From that moment on, life as you knew it, was and will never be the same.

"To Know "

I expected you to be loved by all whom I brought into our space

Never did I imagine I would lose you or I had taken you to such a dreadful place

At that time, in my naiveté state of mind

All I heard him say was, "To you and I he would be kind."

Feeling so unwanted by those that I loved

I thought he came into our lives being sent from heaven up above

He offered me kindness and love for both of us

Instead he showed a way; I would never have thought would be so unjust

I didn't know it was something I should look for in him or anyone else

You were a baby and back then I didn't see that also in my self

Thinking all I had to do was love, feed, wash, and take you wherever I go

I was devastated after reading the report of how he broke your little bones

I trusted he would treat you as well as I saw him treat his own

Instead, I came to learn he caused you harm whenever my back was turned

I can't imagine what you must have felt

I think of each time he hurt you and I never saw a welt

He must have smothered your every cry for help

I felt I kept you so close when did he ever get the time

Had I known I would've fought to my death for you

Of this I still wonder, it will never leave my mind

My thought, take me instead

I wouldn't have been missed, no one I knew would have even cared

God said to me, had I been the one he had taken

Imagine the suffering life with them she would now be living

At first, I thought it was all about me being punished

Somehow, I saw it being the same reason for which I was banished

I now believe, through faith and how God shines in me, I was wrong

At some point through it all, to God I was drawn

Drawn to His home the place where you now exist

Who am I to question why our names are on His list?

I know I am ...

"I Love You"

On the day you came along

I knew right away I had to be none other than strong

The days of being carefree

Were only now to become a memory to me

I wanted right away to shelter and comfort you everyday

No more than one decade and six years old

Bringing new life, "You're too young," I had been told

Once you were bestowed upon me I loved you from the top of my soul

You gave life new meaning to me right away

I started planning on our life together that very same day

I imagined you being in my arms us looking into each other's eyes

I never imagined your words I love you to me would mean goodbye

The time we shared was much too short

No one can believe to save your life, how hard I had fought

Begging and pleading with a soulless and deceitful scoundrel

Who manipulated and led me into taking you into his dreadful world

I knew from the start you were my responsibility

And besides that the only one who would love me just for being me

I would have, without a doubt, saved you from the pain

While sparring myself from everyone's words and looks of disdain

I certainly wasn't sure if I was worthy,

To have heard the last words you said that night to me,

But if it weren't for that Blessing from God

You said your first whole sentence; it made me so proud,

I know without it I never would have made it this far

I hear it every day as clear as one sees a bright shining star

"I love you," I said, as motherly and as dearly as I should

"I love you," You replied, with a sense of articulation in your words

The last words you spoke to me

And those are the words, after being wrongfully judged by most, I use to keep me free.

Free of guilt but I will always feel sorrow

Free of the emptiness as I wait to see you tomorrow

"I Love you," and then …

"Crazy Me"

If it were me, I would go crazy

That's what you offered

I tried, I talked to myself

I talked and talked

I walked in circles and within myself I fought

To GO CRAZY

Just as you said, "If it were me."

I heard it all day long

If it were me, was now my new song

If it were me, was not helpful at all

If it were me, sent me into a fetal position

Screaming, rolling like a marble down a never- ending hall

Words to soothe my pain, if it were me, was not.

If it were me, crazy me, that's not what I got

It wasn't you

It was me and God carries me through the pain

It was me and he made sure I didn't go crazy

Through Him I persevered and still am sane.

I would hug you and ask God to sustain you through your pain,

If I were you.

CHAPTER 11

The freedom to live after telling

We the victims must find our new selves after the suffering we have endured or continue to endure. Each day, my goal is to be a better person than I was the day before. Knowing I am better than I was yesterday brings happiness to the people who love me. To be where I am today is none other than a miracle, "I was lost but now I am found." In my world there is no time for self-pity, but I have all the time for an appreciation for self—Exaltation!

I am to know I am…

A product of God! Not perfect. Molested. Physically abused. Raped. Mother who has lost a child. Cheater. Sister of a murderer. Cheated on. Discriminated against. Whole. A Cast away. Verbally abused. Judged. Estranged. Widowed. Saved. Blessed. Loved. NOT ALONE, only sometimes lonely.

He didn't promise it would be easy but He did promise I would not be alone. He shall not forsake me!

"Free, I Choose Me"

I will not allow you to take my balance

Not spiritually, physically, nor emotionally

My balance is my core

It tells me my purpose; I am here to love me

So within me, my balance I do store.

You took from me that which you had no right

Now I get to tell of all the evil you did almost every night

And now replenished with wholesome thoughts, strength, and a smile on my face

I write to be rid of you and free myself of your disgrace

Before you seemed so big and scary

Now I pity you, and your existence to me as I put pen to paper diminishes through me telling my story.

"Will"

To all of my loved ones Dear, here, and far away.

I take this moment to speak of a gratitude in me that is here to stay.

You must know this is something I always feel and do not express to you every day.

When morning comes and my conscience tells me I am still here, I then take the time to picture your face

Because in my heart for you there is a very special place.

Although these images come one thought at a time

Know that each of you is right here daily on my mind.

I think of what you did or said to me the hours before

I find the love in whatever we did or said and seal it to my core.

This love you show by dialing my number, texting, e-mailing to me, or simply having me in your thoughts

It turns into the energy I need for me to survive and is something that I know, can't ever be bought

The strength to open my eyes every day when God does will

Comes from all of you and with warmth, because of that, my heart does fill

My want to be better at being a person that loves you back in every way

Is what makes me speak of this gratitude within me, which will forever stay.

So again, I take this moment to thank God for sending you here to love me in your own special way!

I have so much to thank my family for. They are always apologetic for not recognizing the signs of my victimization; some have no doubt endured their own pain. Together we are stronger than most. We have our ups and downs but in the end we are always together in heart and soul! I love my family!

Through it all, I appreciate who I am today. I understand and I am at peace with the woman I have become. Each day, God's light shines within me diminishing more and more of the darkness that hangs over me.

"Plant a New Seed"

If I hadn't seen all of the darkness I have seen

What would this life I live to me mean

All the tears I've cried in my times

Helped me learn to appreciate what is mine

My pain is what made me appreciate the value of a good day

If it were not, what on earth would I now have to say.

To overcome is the ultimate gift

I get to put what I don't need on paper and watch Karma shift

Send the darkness back from whence it came

Forcing the culprit to wear his shirt of shame

I write to heal myself and for those who have been where I've been

Hoping to sprinkle some of my courage like rain in the wind

Spreading the gift of my healing all around the world

Knowing that my childhood abuse stories are being told

Read my stories for yourself and to all

We can stand together to break down that disgusting wall

Its silence we do not need

To harvest that un-Godly seed

Take that stance and feel empowered by letting it go

Plant your new seed of freedom and watch yourself grow.

There is a saying, "Even if you've never had it, you still can miss it."
I believe we should never give up on love. It is the main source of

our emotional being, like water is essential to our bodies so is love essential to our emotional stability.

When I use the term love, I don't see it to have any harmful meaning behind it. When two people decide they are so in love, they would like to commit themselves in marriage to one another; I believe there should be an understanding, they do not belong to each other as property but they are united as one through love. Somewhere along the line, there has been a misconception between possession, obsession, and marriage—the unity through love. This misconception has led to countless violent acts of assaults and murders. If there is violence, *it is not love!* With all that has happened, good and bad, I have learned Love truly is …

"I Do"

To Love you unconditionally is to make sure I can trust me

Trust me, with the possibility of having to set you free

Encouraging you if or when your dreams change

Even if it means our relationship doesn't stay the same

Always being a friend to you

Trusting that I can trust me to show this is about your comfort level too!

Making sure each day,

I become a better person even if you do not wish to stay

Trusting myself to always have your best interests at heart

Making sure I show this to you right from the very start

Accepting you for you

And not picking at your flaws whether they are several or a few.

Lifting you up with words, looks, and touches

Never to smother your thoughts, your feelings or wishes

You will know this love is true,

When I show the way I love me, is the way I will always love you.

It is a feeling—your feeling. Not a piece of paper with a title of ownership. A great feeling is *love*. It is a gift to be able to pass that feeling to another and a gift also to receive it. I believe feelings are contagious. When I think about "love" I get all mushy inside, I start smiling, sometimes I cry because I become so overwhelmed with the warmth it expels in my soul. *"It is not self-seeking" (1 Corinthians 13:4).*

"Circle"

Sharing space, greeting mornings during Thanksgiving, face to face

Daily displeasures, whenever frustrations, exhaling them out,

The comfort of leaning on shoulders, openly shedding tears

Intimacy, love, companionship, that's what it's all about.

Caring in ways never to be thought of,

In its entirety, there isn't a moment of doubt

Never to ask, preparation for now and then needs

The circle of true love

Given, care and compassion, harvesting plasmatic seeds

Catch before the fall

Not existing, sense of reproach but an aroma of mind at ease

You too will sacrifice it all

A tall refreshing glass made from humility filled with self not seen,

Sits on the coaster not of cork, love instead.

Decisions made, strengthened by two

Of spirit, connate, truistic emotions had been bred

Words not always spoken, felt, never to fade

Circle of life, true love made.

I do not lack trust in myself. I say this because I am a believer and my trust is my faith in God. When I met my husband, many different people, many different times, told me, "Don't do it Amanda." I understood why they wanted to discourage me, with his one failed marriage, two children from that marriage, now in the midst of ending a relationship with a live-in girlfriend and a newborn child; I surely understood their concerns. What they were missing was the story behind it all and the real person behind the exterior he wore on a daily basis. He was gentle, loving and hopeful in true love as I was. He and I became trusted friends from distrustful hearts, bearing so many scars. We knew we could offer each other the type of comfort, stability, and security needed in both of our lives and we loved each other for those reasons. Some people say, "Behind every successful man there is a strong woman." This may be true but what I would like to add is, we are like engines, give it the right fuel keep it oiled and you should get the best out of it! "A woman's strength depends on the type of encouragement she receives from the man she is working with "side by side!" We were a great team; he needed stability, I offered that. I needed to feel safe and he made sure I was always safe. His name was Fermin S. "Sonny" Archer Jr.

"Men of Me"

I was not the first and regrettably you will not be the last.

Our voices being heard is good but we need to do more to break this cycle of what's still to come and the cycle of our past.

Hear these words men of me.

We are more than death, we are life. More than to be beaten, looked upon with lust, more than pleasure boxes we are the mothers of future generations, fixers, nurturers.

We deserve your respect, protection, and your trust.

Called names in your songs, groped, shot, taken by force, sold, killed, ruined as though we are nothing. Weathering all, because we are and do love.

Bringing life, made of your rib. Standing next to, behind,

before and for you offering peace of mind.

We do deserve your respect, protection, and trust.

We have brought present generations including you and will bring generations to come into the world. A mother in one way or another is what we are, our trust and belief in you is what you neglect to see.

Our stamina to fight, digging deep down in our souls.

To be what we are, what is, what we should be seen as, with your disgraceful descriptions of us in your songs or words openly spoken on the street amongst each other, you stole.

Men of me …

In your rhymes, whores and bitches because we give you the

honor of scratching your itches or not.

Our fight is so hard, the need to be.

We fight to structure families.

Doomed when you are overcome by your shortcomings and your low self-esteem.

Still we Love you men of me. Fight with you, what strength is left.

We go out into the world where we are seen as less.

Not equal, muster up more strength to be respected as whom and what I know I am … A lady.

We deserve your respect protection and trust.

If you won't give it to us where does that leave your Queens, Men of Me.

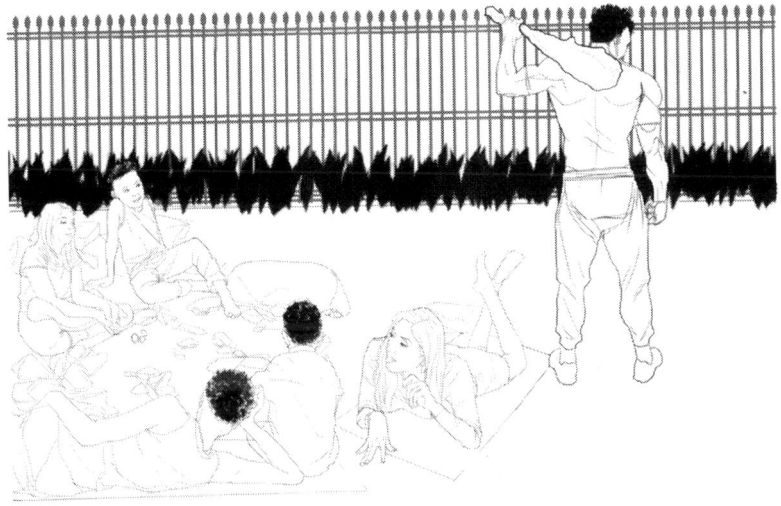

It was great while it lasted. I now find myself without him...

The loss of a loved one is exactly that, "Loss/Lost." Finding the new you without their physical presence takes time. For everyone, the length of time it takes is different. More times than not you feel lost but there is more of you to find, so find it! The new you without. They want us to not just live but to live fully because they love us.

"A Special Place"

I miss you like existing rain would miss falling

Your presence in my space had been thy calling

You not being near, feels like an arrow without aim

I miss you like anything that exists would miss being named

All my thoughts are of you being here

My space is empty without you being near

My days seem longer the time slowly ticks away

I look at the clock and it seems that hour is here to stay

In some ways this is where I had hoped to be

But now I am here and the thing is, I always imagined you'd be here with me.

Finding our way together through the slowdown and the gray

I always thought, as we got old together we would stay

I feel sad always because you are not here

Anger sometimes because I feel some fear

Fear because we had our plan

God showed who is in charge and He took a stand

I watch and wait now not knowing what to do

As days come and go so do my thoughts as I think of you

At the beginning you swore by the moon and the stars up above you'd be there

At the end you asked to be forgiven, our eyes met and I knew we were back to moments we used to cherish and share.

You professed your love for me but at that time I didn't know

What great a love we will always have is what your last words to me will always show

Any doubts of your love for me was erased

For in your heart, for me, I knew you held that special place.

I lost an abundance of emotional security when I lost my husband, Sonny. He is the only man God brought into my life thus far that made me feel safe and comfortable to be who I am and to bare my scars openly. I didn't have to be tough; with him I was able to let my guard down. He was tough for me. His demeanor warranted intimidation but his soul was as gentle as a feather floating in the wind. His friendship and companionship was just what I needed to take a mental break, so I could learn to breathe easy. I know it wasn't easy for him. I miss the security he provided me but more than anything I miss my friend. He always said, we were two perfect bread buns in a basket. Bunn

"Your Smiling Face"

It's amazing and oh so inviting,

The curves that are created on the surface

The indentation on the sides;

The way it leaves footprints in my heart, to all my friends I confide.

The light, inches above that's cushioned by their God-given gloves

Glitters into my eyes, some say it is love.

The Brown surface that surrounds it always would I touch,

So soft and smooth as dark chocolate its creation I know was thought of, no way was it rushed.

People say, from you it's a rare thing to see,

You said, each day you saved it just for me.

The feelings that I get, sometimes bringing tears to my eyes

Tingling in my stomach the strength and thought behind the act not ever to be surmised.

Oh what I would give for a blessing of having it greet me one more time.

Your face with a smile and that glitter in your eyes

I was blessed to have you tell me it was all mine

What I would do to see your smiling face once again,

I shall touch it and tell you, I miss you my love and my best friend.

I miss everyone I have lost—great friends, parents, children, siblings, lovers, and colleagues who are gone physically. Leaving behind cherished memories—sometimes I feel guilty I didn't think of them that moment just before I thought of them. I also know, I would not be able to function normally if my thoughts were consumed with them, yet I want to think of them always. I know now self-preservation is innate, we have bouts of it every day subconsciously. What a *wonderful* and *sovereign* God is He ...

"Everywhere I Go"

I may not say your name everyday

Or talk about you in everything I say

I must admit I don't think of you always

But what I do know is I take you everywhere I go

Just in case I think of you

And those thoughts start to make me blue

You are there, I know it's you because I take you everywhere I go

The memories of your face

The magic of your smile

The warmth and the gentleness of your genuine embrace

These are the memories I use to comfort myself,

This is how I keep you in my space

I take you everywhere, I go

I give all of my love to those who are near

I give them my love withholding my fear

I treasure the moments I have with them also

Hoping the pain of your loss to them I do not show

I mark their presence in my mind as I did yours

My heart has been forever weakened because of your loss

No more pain do I wish to feel but when one loves in one way or another pain is its seal.

Be it through dreams changing, love turning, or as with you, a call from up above.

Regardless, I take you wherever I go my Loves. I take you everywhere I go.

CHAPTER 12

Recovery

How we feel about ourselves and treat ourselves encourages the way we are perceived and treated by others. *We* are beautiful, each of us in our own way.

"In My Own Way"

When I look in the mirror, I don't see myself as a beauty as some may say

look hard when I brush my teeth and wash my face or I'm just looking at myself throughout the day

Sometimes I sit down and my lower stomach easily greets my lap

When I stand in the mirror and look at myself, I can't help but whisper to the mirror "You're a modern-day trap."

I am five-feet two inches in height

And like most women weight gain is sometimes one of my biggest fights

I don't even like going shopping for clothes at the stores anymore

That to me sometimes has now become quite a dreadful chore

Everything I see and think I like

I would put it on, look in that mirror and think it doesn't look right

These are the moments I have after I look at a magazine or a catalog

For some stupid reason for a few moments I would go into a fat fog

Only for a moment though,

Then out of nowhere my face will start to glow

Because when I think of all the woman that I am

I get to thinking; those pictures in those catalogs and magazines are nothing but a mean sham

I would glow so bright it can light up the world

Because at that moment I look up into my soul

A soul full of love, kindness, and laughter

A soul that one can feel touched by from afar

With wide, welcoming wings to shelter you when you're alone or cold

And a smile that will greet you if a gray day ever unfolds

Possessing strengths that are written in the books of great wars and everlasting loves

A soul that continually strives to be as bright as a perfect painted glowing white dove

Who needs to be thin or Coke bottle shaped when they have a personality like mine?

The more I say it; it resonates within me like a glass that is no longer filled with fine wine

All this beauty in me, is exactly what I would then say

I won't ever stop reminding myself, with a big smile on my face,

I am so beautiful in my own special way!

No matter how near or far, there is and will always be a bond between my siblings and I that can never be taken away, not even by death. We have been through a lot, some more than others. Often literally and figuratively, a world apart but always *together* in heart, together forever. My support system has been impeccable! Thank You, Lord.

"Much"

Look at you, moving so glorious, waking the air when you awake

It is enough to you to know that you are of God

The fact that you are here, your existence is proof this is no mistake

Your gracious greetings to everyone

The aura of your presence like a rising sun

If it is not enough for the person you allow into your space

Then they know not the meaning of "Life given only through God's good grace."

Pay attention for those are the ones who are unable to look you in your face.

Look at how far you've come

Carrying your own vibe, majestic to everyone

Being in your presence as God's light shines through you

My sister, look how far you've come.

Never selling yourself short even when it's free

Knowing someone else's less than great interpretation of you

Lacks importance and their envious opinion shall not define thee.

Their words or thoughts shall neither make nor break you

Arrogance, it is not as they say

It is you defining yourself and making your own way

With all of the God-given gifts you possess,

Give no attention, as you continue to pray that they will also be blessed.

You are as important as any other, to so many you are simply wonderful

You have so much to offer to all who want to keep you in their world.

As you sleep you breathe to sustain the act of living without even trying,

Your brain works just fine it tells you to open your eyes when it's time.

Self-preservation, the outstanding mechanism of your body to just function The way it does should leave no room for you to doubt your importance to the world with distinction.

You got up out of your bed that means your motor skills are working

Up in the morning putting on your armor

As you open your eyes and converse with your maker

Getting dressed to go out into the world to play your part

Hoping your good morning to all you greet helps to give them a good start!

Adding into your power bucket all you learn each day

Knowing that smile you give to someone

Can encourage someone to stick around for at least one more day

You live your life knowing, your life given means in God you trust

Your presence in my world, to me, means just as much!

My life is far from perfect. I must say this, I will not use my imperfect life as an excuse to not try to be perfect. What I don't have I can't give, I am happy for what I have been blessed with and believe in sharing my blessings, my love, my ears for listening, my heart, and most of all my experiences. None of which is too small! I am to know I am blessed in so many ways …

"Giving"

Giving is wonderful, I was told when I give I should give wholeheartedly

Give without looking for anything in return give unselfishly

I have heard people say, when I give I feel so good

But isn't that one of the reasons in giving that is understood

In actuality when we give we are giving selfishly

We do want something back

And that in itself is a selfish act

When I give it is because I want to share.

To me it's a sign of showing that I care

A greeting, a compliment, something monetary, forgiveness, or a meal to eat

A card, flower, hug, or a simple rub of aching hands or feet.

I don't know what tomorrow will bring

It's not as though when I die, I can take with me, anything

Don't now take my words as saying you should have it because I want to give

That to me will mean you don't really care how I live

Some people ask not because they need

If ever I am asked, before I give, I ask God to guide me in knowing if it stems from envy, needing, or just plain greed

A person, who gives without wanting anything back, won't wait for someone to ask

If they really care they will save you of that task

Making sure you don't feel anything less than the person you are

They will take note and help because they hear your cry of need in their heart near or from afar

When you give, don't expect anything back, don't speak of it to another and don't put pen to paper with thoughts of keeping track.

Give because you have been blessed with the gift of enough to share,

There's always someone in need and it is a great way to show you care.

I would like my children, our children, to be able to feel confident about themselves and knowledgeable enough to decipher who around them is considered a responsible adult. Someone they can cry out to for help and that person will look out for their best interests. They are our future and this world keeps getting worse. We teach them right from wrong and send them out as prey for the evildoers to confront them. Knowledge is the key to preparedness and preparedness is the key to survival. If I can help it, the element of surprise will be struck down by some of the words I have written about my experiences. I hope all I have shared in this book helps to break the cycle of stifled emotions and is passed down for generations to come. I love you all!

"Heartbeat"

I want to share with you everything I know and how I know it

I want to tell you every wrong I have done so you don't have to experience it

I want you to know everything about the big and small mistakes I've made

So you can choose either to bypass them or make them and learn from them as I did

All of my experiences—good, bad, or indifferent are what makes me, me.

Some of them, huge scars I will take throughout the rest of my journey

I know I can't shield you from the challenging things you must go through

Even if I could, I most definitely am not sure I would want to.

I cherish every experience I've ever had, they are my foundation to all of what I am today,

This foundation my life has been built upon was already written, believers in God would say.

I wish all great things for you

As your mother, the thought of you even stumbling can make me blue.

But as I did when you were a child

I gave you space to build your own resistance to the hardships of this world, knowing that could take a while.

Standing in the background with words of guidance, encouragement, love, a kiss, a hug, or just silence if needed.

Making sure I am there whether you fail or succeed.

All of life's challenges that you must face

For you, all these years I prayed for God's good grace.

I understand I can't be there for you all of the time

But I hope my teachings to you will forever stay in your mind

If by chance you were too busy trying to find your way

Were just overwhelmed building your foundation or by things led astray

Perhaps missed what I've told you many times before

Know that each day by me, you are loved more and more.

We all know pain can be felt emotionally and physically. When it is physical pain, most of the time we know there is some type of remedy; but when it's emotional it is more difficult to render the type of help needed. Too often, a person won't reach out for help and sometimes although we see they are suffering, we respect their privacy. Sometimes we don't see, not because we don't want to but because we are tied up in our own world. After my husband passed away, I knew there were many people affected by his death, including myself. I knew most of all, our children and his father would have to learn to accept the loss of their father, and his father's only son. As much as I tried to be in-tune with their grieving process, there were things I missed. We are all still grieving in our own way but with God in our lives and with love we are finding our new normal. Talking with each other helped tremendously, and we are more comfortable and healthier now speaking about our loss.

"I See You"

Your actions wave at the world

It is loud and clear

You wait to hear

To feel the closure of the space in between you and not just anybody

You scream when you gaze at the world

Your soul is so fired up, everything you do with fiery blaze

Asking but without asking, begging with your head turned away

For the comfort of maternal

Arms stretched out as you lash out for the belonging

Wanting but not wanting the good from the bad

Crying without tears, wanting to be a part or a piece

From there not here but not just anywhere

Every mark you place on yourself, the pain leaving a stain to remember

The hurt inside, closeted but pounding from within

Your soul, sole comfort needed, not wanting the loneliness

Heaving to be seen your inner cry, from there not here

But here, you don't, I do see you.

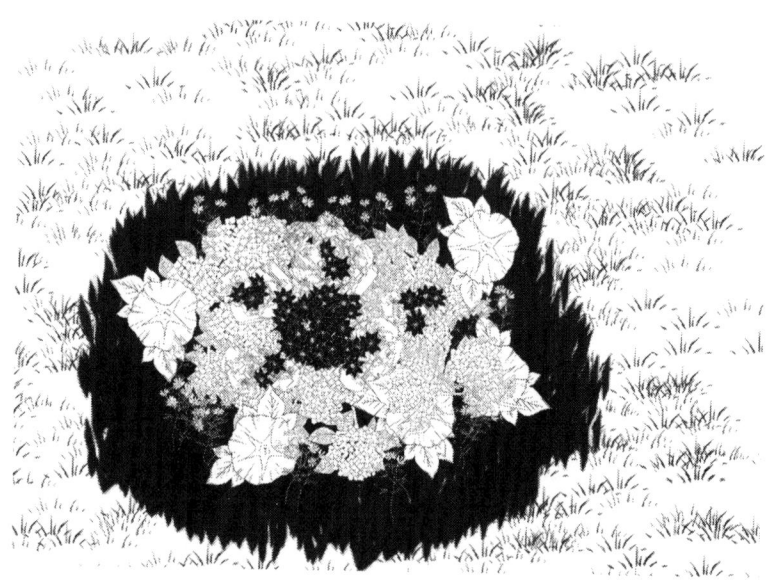

The things we sometimes take for granted. Who are we to think, we should take anything for granted? We are selfish creatures until we are no more—Don't wait.

"Wonders of the World"

The wind blows, the temperature drops; the sky gets gray;
The smell of the air, at its arrival even changes.
The light dims, inside I feel vulnerable and very sensitive,
I am not sure why.
The feeling of comfort food, my favorite blanket comes to mind and
a nice cup of hot chocolate just at that moment would be fine.
TV on or not, the melody of emotional softness overcomes me;
My thoughts go deep into a place, at that moment, where I really
would like to be.

A flash of sadness, the beauty of all the materials I have surrounded myself with

I feel so alone, quite aware I am not, yet still a sense of feeling lonely as I sit,

Looking out of the window anxiously awaiting the arrival of that sound

Leaves swishing back and forth in the wind, the sound of everything else seems to have lessened.

Send me a sign that you are close, closer than I hope; now everything seems to be slowing down.

My anxiety grows, this intense waiting; I smell you in the air.

I wish you were here already; I will sit here and look at you with wonder.

You are mystifyingly beautiful, the reason for your existence is so clear.

I most certainly will reach out and touch you, dance as you touch my skin.

Smell you; open my hands so I can feel your touch, are you near?

Show me a sign that you are near.

One speck please, you are the source of life within.

I hear you, the pitter-patter of your sure arrival, soon to be a splash on the sill

The company you bring

The calmness you bring within, a sense of cleanliness, a change of mood.

I feel you on my face and through my hair on my fingertips.

Drip, drop, drip, drop and a crisp roaring sound of the many fast drip drops all around. You're here, now I feel so tingly inside! Hello Rain …

The mind can be a dangerous thing when you are in despair. There are times my thoughts can take me so far and then times they take me nowhere. I know with all I have endured and who knows what's to come, I must not allow my thoughts to linger in either too long. Then it would have all been for naught. "Snap out of it and keep moving!", is what my subconscious self says to me. And so, I do—snap out of it until the next time!

"In My Head"

I now know where you come from

Rushing in, making my thoughts flood

Rolling around my in head

Feeling everything as I think them, I fight for you not to spread

Nerves fluttering, blood rushing, things inside me squirming like worms.

What you do to me when the time comes, is not fair

Rhythm so loud I think my heart is in my ears

Doubts of my existence for the morrow as I toss and turn night after night

Pacing back and forth without any explanation in sight

Fighting to not be overcome by you, that is what I dread

Go back where you came from taking over my thoughts, then and there you are boss of the cloud in my head

I push back with every thought I have with all of my mental strength

I can feel you fighting back as strong as ever to stay your path at length

I wrestle with you, to persevere, must shake you

Not just today, shake you off until you are far away

Put you in a box and mail you to someplace you will forever stay

Sanity, by this my fight against you is led

You swim around in my gut, my jaws hurt, teeth clenched

You come when you want to, you make me question things and myself, you are all in my head

I stand up against you once and for all

I know where you come from

I created you, piece by piece, thoughts topped by more thoughts.

I talk you out, how I destroy you, I talk and I breathe instead

Fear, anxiety replaced with faith and belief in myself

There shall be no more of you, no more unwelcoming thoughts ever to dwell in my head.

I'm not sure exactly when I knew what it meant to believe in God. What I do know is believing in Him is what took me away from where I was, what brought me to where I am and believing in Him will take me where I need to be always! I know "I am", because I "Trust in God!"

"Closer to You"

I cry, I smile, and I tremble

When I think of the many times you kept me from falling each time I stumbled.

You give me something new each time I experience a loss

Be it physically, emotionally, or in monetary cost.

I get tired in thoughts and in making my way

Sometimes wanting to hopelessly give it all up but in the blink of an eye you bring me to a new and better day.

My mind and my heart I have opened to you

Now with every step I take toward making things right

You show me a better life is what I am due

At the end of my tired day

I lay down my head and I pray

That your gift to me when I am awake,

Is to be closer to you; for this my, heart surely aches.

Sometimes I get so impatient with my emotions, especially when I am down. I often pray about it, wanting the bad feelings to go away quickly. My faith tells me, "It's going to get better. I believe it's going to get better but it never seems to come quick enough. I can't imagine how I will make it to tomorrow. Then I make it through many tomorrows and look back at where I came from—It does get better! It is better! I am to know, everything happens in God's time.

"Still"

Stay covered; don't move that will be most of the day today

Think, think, think but no action

To know it is good sometimes just to be still

How long though, should someone stay this way?

Too much of one thing, it has been said, is good for nothing

One day comes and another on the bed just lay

The day that follows, you don't want to but again you to stay

No light, to see anything in front of you to calculate the meaning of them

The heart is nowhere to be found, the energy is in the distance

And the mind is too lethargic to find from whence this does stem

So sudden, or was it slowly creeping, unnoticed?

This can't be good, something or someone in your mind proclaims

How long is the will going to be like this?

Roll, sigh but listen to the stillness that speaks

Fight and fight, open that curtain see the daylight

It is a gift to be awakened, and pushing back is its payment

This earth and all of its contents shall be inherited by the meek

When it is done, found in reserve must be the will to live,

To love, give, and replenish so to endure

Two days maybe three, it's okay the mind, heart and soul

They too, should be allowed the time needed to be restored

So then, be over with this until the time comes again,

As being demands tis the time to be still.

No one can make us happy. We have to do it for ourselves. Be happy with ourselves, and then we can experience the bonus of someone adding to our happiness. It is said, "emotions are contagious". I think we should all take a moment to ourselves and ask: "Self, what are some of the things you like? Who are you? Do I like myself? If you don't get to know yourself, how or why would anyone want to get to know you?"

"My Purpose"

Confused, was what I was.

What was or is my purpose in life?

So many things I felt I wanted to do and did

Especially now that I am no longer a wife

Days of sorrow turned into years of the saddest tomorrows.

What was, is, or will be my purpose I thought?

It wasn't the ring, the paper, the title, or the cooking.

For, now in my life, without you I feel there is so much I was missing

I miss the talks and the ice cream walks,

The Friday night ordering with the kids and the Pepitone Pizza takeouts;

The grump you were when the kids were misbehaving

The childish sounds you made when I wouldn't give in

Purpose in life, my own.

Without you, I never thought I would,

But since you've been gone, oh my, I have grown.

Although away from each other before you departed,

Those vows we took, were so true with love,

Our togetherness was as sure as when we first started.

Holding onto every memory and to things you left behind

I heard you say in my ear each day going forward,

"I will always be sorry," is what I hear in my mind.

Be as nice to yourself as I was to you.

Open your heart for those special things allowing someone in again,

You deserve and should have another love just as true.

I smile more than I cry now.

Acceptance of your loss, time passing did allow.

I live and I give, I love more than I can ever believe.

I laugh at the big things, sometimes cry at the little things.

I even realize, myself I did deceive,

Through my misconception of the phrase I had once been given,

"A person comes into one's life for a reason, a lifetime or a season."

I know now we can sometimes be all three

Those three seasons are really all about me

I am my purpose in my own life, I am the only one that can make me happy.

I believe, being in love is a feeling I would miss even if I never had the experience to have someone I was in love with. *"Love is patient, love is kind. It does not envy, it does not boast. It is not proud. It is not rude, it is not self-seeking, it is not easily angered, it keeps no account of wrongs. Love does not delight in evil but rejoices with the truth. It always protects, always trusts, always hopes, always perseveres." 1 Corinthian 13:4-8*

"Together"

I am comforted by not just his touch but also his presence in my life

To be shown I am his priority,

Knowing with every passing moment he notices something special about me

He thinks about how my day is going when we're apart

Appreciating the way I look when he opens his eyes each morning

Expressing to me in many ways, I am the reason his days always have such a good start

He prays with and for me each and every day

He takes care of me tenderly and stands by my side always

At that time of the month, with his hands, my stomach he does soothe

Creating music in his head to hum because my presence in his life keeps him in a good mood

Asking me to dance while in my eyes he constantly stares

Picking me up when I am down and feeling bleak

A man whose loving heart for me will forever skip a beat

Sensing when I need a hug or just a look of assurance that he is there

Who's so in tune with me, from a distance he can sense my despair

Hugging me just because and finding my angry face sexy

Never hurting me intentionally, willing to listen when I don't speak

Reading my actions, no matter what they are

We are so blessed to experience how wonderful it feels to be together

Holding the open umbrella, he shows his hand is never to full for me

Dances in the rain, playing in the snow, and sometimes just to see me smile he acts foolishly.

Being himself, holding back on nothing he does or says

Taking my feelings into consideration even when we are having a bad day.

Willing to stand firm for himself, times when I am wrong

Demonstrating manhood with no resentment of my personality being strong

Being serenaded, he brings tears to my eyes because he can't sing

Accepting me for who I am, that person who loves him just the same

We wait in anticipation of what wonders our tomorrows will bring, together.

Yet still, here they come, one by one trying to victimize us in one way or another. When I say they, I speak of the people whose cups are already filled with husbands, wives and children yearning for and deserving of the love and trust due to them. The unappreciative, greedy enough to have it all and still wanting more people.

Selling false hopes—having what most of us would like to have. I would like to have that type of love but I am not in the market for false anything. I know my worth. Not just for the sake of saying "I have a man."

Some women buy it with their innermost need for that love.

It hasn't been easy being the recipient of all those scars but "I am" and "I know I am" to be *loved* not just by anyone but that someone God sees as fit and worthy. I *love* and *respect* Me!

"Alone"

Where has it all gone?

The innocence and fun of meeting that special someone.

The excitement of seeing the new face

And knowing just by the feeling you get from having them in your space

They are the one.

Instead you see them and feel a tingle

But because of the dreadful games that have been introduced to society you somehow imagine it is better to stay single

Where has the sense of courting, romance, laughter, and commitment to loving another, now gone?

That a person feels the need to fulfill their lives with, when they are single and have no one

Men presenting themselves to single women

Even though they have someone at home waiting to romantically greet them

Women selling themselves short by knowing these men have families at home but still entertaining their advances

Little do they know, for true love, they are ruining their chances

We are the women that make up this society

So by selling ourselves short and entertaining the possibility of committing adultery we are adding to our own misery

We're demonstrating, to destroy a marriage is acceptable while saying to ourselves—"He loves me more than her, so he won't do the same to me."

But really what it's showing is his unfaithful capability.

See, the miseries to come with that package is like throwing a dog a bone

So you win him, is how you shall lose him

And at the end, likelihoods are, in your heart you will still end up feeling alone.

Despite it all, I have so much love, laughter, and life left inside of me I would like to share. So many wonderful things to experience, but we, whomever the next love for me is and myself, must be patient.Everything in God's time, to have the privilege of being together to share it with each other.

"In Time "

I yearn to be with you and feel your touch

I know in our world of love that's not asking too much

I need to feel the warmth of you on my skin

This I once said and was assured I will not have to say it again

The feeling you bring when I am with you

The feeling that we are one together and never again to be two

I think of us together and in my mind

*I am assured, no matter what type of storm our love shall weather
for, it is one of a kind*

You make me feel I am all there is in this world

*That look in your eyes when you look at me, tells of a wonderful
love story for years have been told*

Told in the books of love everlasting

That all others dream of someday having

Dreaming to have, not ever wanting to let go of

That love they know they won't have enough of

In this love there is no such thing called smothered

There is only us wanting to be alone with each other

During the times we must step away

That built in security our love provides, lets us know this love shall never be frayed

Glowing and smiling when we are apart as though we are right next to one another

Reflecting on the moments we shared and will share again together

Being without you right now causes me no fear

Because I feel in my soul, I am missed, by you even though our love for each other is not yet here.

CLOSING

The greatest of them all!

"Love"

Simple it is not, energy in its sparse but genuinely ample form,

Sleepless nights filled with thoughts, warms your heart

Effervescent anxiety permeates the moments to your day's start.

Waking in the arms, or not, maybe an arm's slide away to the morning touch.

Satisfaction in space sharing.

Outweighing discomforts of undisguised, bland, and neutral reality of one's true being.

To be loved or loving someone in this way.

No trudging to conquer the world, challenges barely found when love finds it place.

Strengthening, gratifying, and needed by all it is.

No status, title, or wealth need be, when true.

A delight to give and to have,

Pushes through darkness enhanced by truth

Grows with the light, creates unbreakable knots

Foundations formed by waves of trials themed with compassion at its root.

Misunderstood by nonbelievers, misread by hypocrites.

Too expensive to be marketed so precious to all, desired.

It is everything for nothing when nothing means more than everything

Creeps up when least expected, painful when rejected

Often hungered for, so desired; often used to deceive

In its true form always a pleasure to give or receive.

Love.

I end this part of my journey knowing I am free, happy, not alone, and working to make myself happier and better each day, through God's endless mercies.

He made me who and what I AM.